CONTENTS

THE WILL OF GOD IN YOUR LIFE

CHAPTER 1
WELCOME INTO LIFE
WORLD DISTRACTION
MASTERING LIFE
THE PHYSICAL BODY
CHAPTER 2
CHAPTER3
THE REALITY OF THINKING AND IMAGINATION
KNOWING THYSELF
HOW DO WE KNOW OURSELVES
LAWS OF NATURE
SEARCHING FOR WISDOM
THE JOURNEY OF NO RETURN
WISDOM
THE BIBLE
MASTERING THE ART OF LIVING
THINKING
REALISING ONES GOALS
ATTRACTING FINANCIAL ABUNDANCE
BETTER HEALTH
THE LORD IS MY CONFIDENCE
WORK YOURSELF TO GET WHAT YOU NEED
CONDITIONALITY POWER IN US
COMMUNICATION WITH NATURE
GLORIFICATION TO GOD
EXPERIENCE
EXERCISES FOR THE MIND
LIVING WITHOUT THINKING
LIFE IS BIGGER
NATURAL LAWS OF LIFE
THINGS THAT MAKE US DERAIL FROM THE TRUE
PURPOSE OF LIFE
DISEASE
ANXIETY

DISSAPPOINTMENT
FEAR
SELF-CONDEMNATION
HIGH SENSITIVINESS
GENEROSITY
SUCCESS
THIS BOOK IS ONLY FOR MEN
FRIEND / TRUST

THE WILL OF GOD IN YOUR LIFE

Chapter 1

WELCOME INTO THE LIFE

Everyone at birth is given a lifetime opportunity. How good and how well one makes use of it depends on the training and awareness one has had. Very early in the process of growing up, children are imbued with a lot of compelling notions that some things are not what they are and can never be changed. But simply because they have been told that those things are true does not necessarily mean they are.

Belief systems that are inculcated into majority from youth always impose a lot of limit on the child's judgment about life and to new ideas. These barriers are the causes of a lot of misjudgments and disbeliefs derailing a lot of children.

Although parents may sometimes succeed in guiding the curiosity of their wards, they can never suppress their abilities to think the way they want and this is why some children who have decided to go for the truth are labeled deviants or bad. When parents limit the exploration tendencies of their children they are selling them out to the coziness of sub human conservatism.

The mind of a man can only develop when he relaxes himself from anxieties of life relating to problems of staying alive called fear; things have to get worse before they can get better. A man without experience in life is not occupied with the most urgent and necessary demands of living.

We have to explore and investigate to stabilize. Then it is only then that we can expand our awareness and understanding both of ourselves and that of the complex environment we are living in.

Sophisticated man has made simple things complex out of their own elaborate confusion, a man who gives his all is as stupid as the man who gives nothing.

It becomes impossible to teach a man how to use his sense of perception if his belief system has been crippled by his parents, our minds is the energy structure that we have, to guide and guard us consciously and unconsciously for better for worse. When someone plants a seed and allows it to grow into a tree, without trimming the tree,

Will keep on growing in all directions, growing deep roots spreading out taking all the nourishment from the ground on which it is planted.

Right and wrong are man made precepts. What is right in one part of the world may be totally wrong in another. Experience is the name given to men past mistakes. Receiving a new truth is always adds a new sense.

There is no adventure on earth like exploring one's own mind. All life is mysteries but the man is a slave when he refuses to solve mysteries even though some mysteries can never be solved.

Majority of the people in the world wish and crave to have knowledge but only a few are ready to pay the price, life is a series of ups and downs, to which life always returns for everything we loose, we gain something.

Youth is a time for exploration, a time for experimentation for change, a time to revolt. The child sees the world for the first time and thinks it to be a bed of roses, for the first time they have to demand to discover the world for themselves. It is only if they are exposed to the many frauds and deceit in all areas of life, the abundant illusions that the establishment of a new social order will be found out. A lot of trials and errors based upon love hate and other noble sentiments called principle.

Adults over complicate very simple matters thereby misleading their children and because children are dependent on their parents initially they are already poor because they possess no reason for satisfaction and freedom to think their own ideas which is their vast empires where and with which they would have lived happily, now become anxiety and unrest for them, they are now made to hide behind a façade or wall of cynicism. All creative acts involve a certain degree of risk. Nothing seeked nothing found, nothing ventured nothing won.

In this life there are some people who can only develop in company of others, and others who have to retire to solitude.

Man is a spirit a creature of another world and it is only when he can become free from the bounds of the flesh that he can roam the world as a spirit and then help others by thought.

What people do not realize is that life on earth is but an illusion, a testing place, and a school for us to learn. Death is birth, dying is merely the act of being born in another place of existence called paradise or hell regarding the state of mind of the person involved. Man or the spirit of man is eternal the body of man is a temporary garment that clothes the spirit.

Between you and God life is not survival of the fittest but between man and man life is survival of the fittest. The prosperity of the generous man never fails while the miser finds no comforter. Let the powerful man be generous to the suppliant. Let him look down the long path of lives for life is like a ball and anywhere you stand upon is the middle of the world.

The wind that blows is all the body feels do not try to control life. Life is greater and stronger than individual destiny you may fall, life may beat you, it may be hard on you but do not ever try to control life, live it live life. Being straight with people is what counts. Every man has equal opportunities before GOD.

WORLD DISTRACTION

There are two types of circumstances in the life of a man, circumstances that can be controlled and circumstances that can never be controlled.

If one cannot think seriously he should work seriously, if a man decides to play in the game of living, he must be ready to abide with a set of rules governing that game. Without rules there can never be a game.

A man therefore has a choice; he is free not to play in the game thereby not following any rules and plays the game of life as he wishes or he abides by the rules of living called destiny.

This is life!

We all lead a double life like actors on the stage. As long as there are two roles to be play neither can be real life all of it is fiction.

We creatures of habit hate to have our plans changed.

A wise man always bows to the inevitable. Human nature is doing unto others as you want others to do unto you but most humans are alien not only to themselves but to the human race.

Most men understand where they are but not why. They are too grounded in the world varieties, to know that those obsessed with life will loose it one day. Stupid people can sometimes be positive in that they have little ability to project alternatives. They never know what they are missing and so they are happy. One will be amazed at the people who do without thinking. Educated people! People are blinded by what they are made to believe in.

There is no limit to the stupidity of mankind and to the results of that stupidity. The sum total of the world distractions for man lies in his reasoning for women and love of money. What a world! The world is endlessly amusing, so craving, so weak, so whimpering, so greedy, so exigent, so fearful, and so heedless of history and warnings, so brutal and sentimental with filthy crimes of the body and soul. Anyone who wants peace in this world must be prepared for a lot of insult.

Money is not everything in a man's life nor does his real happiness lie in gathering it but many young people have been made to believe that it is only money that brings happiness and therefore the most important thing in life. People therefore waste their life chasing after vain things while depriving themselves of other things. This mistaken way of thinking has led a lot to their graves. It has led a lot into greed and unrest, it has ordered majority into alienation and sin. They have failed to possess abundance in life; there is sorrow everywhere because the pursuance of money by all means brings no permanent good to anyone. Give men a chance to choose between money and wisdom and what do they do? They choose money and tomorrow when the money is finished they wail and cry.

It is useless to attempt to reason a man out of what he has never reasoned into. Who will wish for an eternal life except a ravenous fool who cannot satisfy his greed?

How long a man lives is not important. Life is surfeited whether the man is young or old it is only how good a man has lived that the beauty of living and gratitude is measured.

There is no limit to the stupidity of man!

Majority of human I meet are docile and dull, rejecting the truth with equal lack of positive reason. They are blind in that they are friends with the world and money, and this makes them an enemy of GOD and the world that they live in.

When we say that truth is simple, it will always be obvious for there is nothing so mysterious and sublime as simplicity and truth. A hunger for love and comradeship is as natural to humans as food and water for the soul.

There is nothing new at all as to the causes of the problems of man it is just that man has refused to make maximum use of all the gifts of nature reserved for them by GOD.

MASTERING LIFE

Many cultures for example have passed myths down to mislead their offspring's and indeed the entire tribe would often participate in the lies governing the myths that the lies have been made to look as truth. Methods and rituals have been designed to alter the state of knowing the truth thus such deception relate importantly to the type of information passed around and brought back to play in the lives of the people for the benefit of the tribe.

Every man is a multi dimensional being and though most people are merely aware of their consciousness, they can only project and control their whims but not fears, it is most important for man in this world to maintain a passive state of mind at all times and to always find happiness because the mystical guides are only willing to help those who help themselves. The true man must go gain experience both advanced and intelligences of the inner realms that talks about the truth.

There are many aspects of life that needs to be experimented with and it is simply a matter of thinking what you want to know that can liberate a man from a lot of bondage governing his life. No pain no gain, no harm can come to a man seeking the truth, a situation cannot occur more than it can happen while experiencing what has been said about that situation.

The bible talks about the fear of God being the beginning of wisdom, if one fears GOD, he will project his consciousness beyond the confines of the five physical senses to assume the truthful role of what life is all about.

Thoughts can often cause what we know as reality fluctuation. Intent is then formed to a definite statement that if I am in the presence of Almighty GOD as it is written about Him how will I believe. The mind and the sub-conscious can then be programmed to succeed. Thus the truth is manifested through GOD's own saying:

> Ask and you shall be given
> Seek and you shall find
> Knock and it shall be opened unto you
> (Matt. 7:7)

What have you been asking about all your life?

What have been seeking?

How many doors of opportunities have you come across and how many times have you knocked upon it?

Starting from these three basic questions you have continuously started to ask the wisdom of GOD to visit you but before embarking upon these important objectives one must make sure he has emotionally commitment with the resolve to achieve the motives he has laid down with compliance with what GOD the ALMIGHTY has passed to us through the bible.

Although a lot of people might say that I know the bible, I read it I know all the verses, how good are you letting your life manifest in the good tidings that the bible has to offer in terms of obedience and not running after things of the world. Our creator GOD is at the very center of all that we do. That no matter how we live the life, once we fear GOD and obey His commandments there is joy and peace. Death no longer poses a threat to one, it is something good to embrace when the time comes.

GOD is pure, rich and spiritual. He has given us all that we need to master the life. We have the physical, mental and spiritual and because GOD is pure all of us are pure in spirit until we loose the awareness of our spirit. As we relax more and more, and incline into the full image of GOD, we come to realize that when we are nearer to GOD, we get comfort.

Our bodies are composed of energy vibrations and nature herself is so good that we can lend from her at all times.

The Physical Body

The energy emanating from the body is so great but it needs only food to supplement and help us to relax. The physical body is made of three parts that are:

- Positive
- Negative
- Neutral

The energy radiating from the body is divided laterally from the middle of the head to the groin. The right side is the positive side while the left side is the negative side and the middle is the neutral.

The body is such in a natural state that a person can determine what they want to do with their life. When a person intentionally wants drastic changes in their lives they have to make use of the three sides for the purpose of the effect they want.

It should be noted however that if you use the wrong side for the change you want to affect, reverse is always the case so you must master your body to know the desired effect or change you desire.

I would like to commence by emphatically stating an important truth which everyone should know. There is really no such state as a failure in life. What most people believe to be failure in life is just a state of mind that has been made manifest in their life to overcome their state of mind, people would have heard about positive thinking. Know thyself.

Although the universe consists of illusions, it is good for the man to always think only in terms of genuine and well pressing needs and never to compare with other people. Sometimes what other people have that we do not have may be a less desirable thing once it manifests into our subconscious. Processing and creating everything we think we need is a GOD given grace that all human possess.

Knowing what we want and desiring are two different things; most desires only bring unhappiness at the end of the day but the immediate wants are those things that will be given in an order of preference.

By constantly making use of positive thinking about a particular desire the longer we continue thinking about it the sooner a divine intervention comes to our aid to get them done for us. Unwillingness to wait for supernatural provisions will only produce tragedies every time. This brings us to the concept of asking and waiting for our requirements.

A lot of people cannot afford to wait so they never wait for the favorable results to manifest in their lives thus, the truth they were supposed to learn becomes what they can never discover. Money does not bring happiness rather happiness brings money. The joy that follows wisdom takes us to heights we have never ever dreamt off existed in our cosmos.

A lot of people can run away from studies that may make their lives better their only thoughts in life are to provide for their greed. In other words things that may bring harm to their fellow humans, things that may bring about the law of redistribution or things that will fade away. Out of the highest degree of manifestation in our lives, deep concentration of energy in the form of thoughts towards our goals is essential.

On an individual level, a person can create his own heaven or hell here on earth, as this is a subconscious process whereby the very basis of things manifest as the object of imagination. Magic in its truest and highest form is a desired result by the magician who has made proper use of universal laws of the universe to overshadow and manifest desired results for his observers. Magic and occult practices for example originate from natural universal laws that bring about effects that people see as miraculous.

The joy of life in the most sacred form depends on the manifestation in the highest forms of influences and other series of actions that make us better our lives.

We once mentioned the three states of man which just like a magnet affects the physical, mental and spiritual. The physical cannot be without the spiritual and mental and vice versa. All have to work as one in accordance, and with expertise with which the individual is able to focus concentration and make the fullest possible use of universal laws of powers of the universe.

Let us take a look at the various levels of development in our world. It should be noted that when we talk about the levels of development, we are talking about individual differences and the highest destiny manifestation in humans.

As human beings are spiritually made in the image of GOD who has created everything from the beginning. The physical human has deviated from the original course from which he was created. Mental sense in the universal continuum has detoriated with the pursuance of earthly gains and this is why meditation, magic and other works of art are considered to be forms of immoral practices.

There are vast sources of energy in the environment that are characteristic to the concept of earth and time. This conditions are transient projections created by the minds of humans that are destined to progress from the path already prepared for us by GOD. It is only a few who tread this path.

I am sure that if these powers were to be made manifested to a lot of people, majority would use it to harm others thus the skills we learn on and off the street are valuable in the sense that the person who can merge the two together for proper use is the achiever. School just teaches us to be able to read and write.

When we fail, we always gain strength for life. The real merit is not in success but in the endeavor, win or loose, failure or success we should be thankful because they test our capabilities of resistance. With them, we are compelled to persevere from the energy of the opposition. When we fail we always gain strength.

Faith and hope are the finest and greatest of all spiritual gifts that work together to force a man from bondage of power and the dead hand of the past, to open for new possibilities of the divine.

When one produces an unduly complicated solution to a problem, he does not have a solution to the problem but has created a new problem. Problems dilemmas and paradoxes are not sources of discouragement and frustrations but the necessary spurs of new knowledge and creativity. If you want to learn you go to school or you don't learn.

Chapter 2

A road is truly two roads in one to truly see it, you have to see it going and coming

No matter how far you have gone on a wrong road, turn back. The wild boar runs away from the tiger knowing fully well that each being endowed by the power of nature with deadly strength may kill the other. By running it preserves its life and that of the tiger. This is not cowardice it is love of life.

The universe is abundantly enriched with wealth or anything we desire but most people are one minded organs and do not simply realize their natural GOD's given ability to possess what they desire. Majority of the people only believe that things exists solely because we can see them but this is not so everything exists because of everything and because most people do not actually know what they desire, they never have experience in terms of greed for what they actually desire.

The life herself is full of abundance of air; water; nature life etc and one needs not contemplate his desire in life and think towards it before he can be an achiever. It is always necessary to meditate on desires and consider to what fulfillment the desire will be made used once we get it. What one really want is as important as that thing we want if we want to get it.

If ideas tend to realize themselves in our desires then it is really important for man to have a right kind of ideas in his mind.

Whatsoever things are honest, lovely, pure and of good virtue should be things we should desire. Every man is a sun until they stop themselves from shinning and because people are dependent on others, they will always be poor not realizing that thoughts are vibrations and can be used to create something more permanent in their lives. Every individual can create his own heaven or hell right here on earth.

Chapter 3
The Reality of Thinking and Imagination

Within the innermost sphere of thinking and imagination, things desired are brought into instant manifestation through thoughts to become a reality. This is a natural process that needs no school or education because before anything can manifest into the physical, it must first be in thought form, which is interacted or preceded by imagination.

Thinking and imagination work hand in hand for manifestation to take place. Knowledge drives away ignorance, whosoever that does not know the meaning of what he/she reads, says or wants or is here to do on earth is an ignorant person insofar as much as what he/she reads, says, wants or is here to do on earth is pointing at him/her. GOD will never destroy the world to create another Adam and Eve.

Most people dance around in a circle and suppose the truth we all know. Life on earth is but an illusion, a testing place, a school, knowledge of man's behavior and endurance to test their adversity. What amazes me on earth is meeting everyday of my life with senseless people here on earth asking senseless questions all over and over.

One time I was in Tripoli Libya, I took a taxi and as the driver was driving, he suddenly exclaimed "Duniya Garba" without anybody talking to him. I was right beside him in the front of the cab and was surprised of the obscene word he had used to describe the world.

What prompted him to use the obscene word I guess I will never know because no man on earth can directly experience the consciousness of another? The only consciousness we can directly influence and have direct and immediate knowledge of is our own; one can only know the consciousness of other beings indirectly.

The word "Duniya" means world while "Garba" in Arabic language means prostitute.

Why this man voiced out his opinion of the world in his hard bent anger as the world is a prostitute may be after looking at the man who was around my age in his own country maybe not married perhaps with no shelter of his own, no privacy and he had to be a taxi driver, a scoundrel cheating innocent people charging exorbitant prices only to go back to his mechanic to spend everything for repairs all over and over.

I could be wrong this is just my thinking and I felt very sorry for him. I responded in my African latent voice in Arabic "Sadiq,

Mush, Duniya Garba, Nas gad bil duniya garba" he was surprised because he definitely must have known that I was a foreigner and will not understand what he had just exclaimed so when I replied him I saw awe and shock on his face. Although he saw the truth in my response I could see him elated as he smiled. What I just told him in Arabic was that it was not the world that was bad but the people who inhabit the world are the ones we should call Garba. In such a few words he agreed with me because he saw a lot of reason in what I had just told him.

The sun that shines today is the same sun that has been shining since my greatest grandfather was born and will still be shining when my last great great grand children shall pass away, the moon also. There might be variations in the weather during one day.

Humans label the days, seven days a week, twelve months a year and give each name in arithmetical order apparently each day is not different from the last one but activities differ.

To a man, what happened today in activities may be different to what he will do tomorrow but the sun and the moon will always rise and set in the same direction.

Life! Life! Why do we all struggle in the toils of doubt?

The confrontation scene "life" meets you, Virtue vanquishes vise.

Life! More or less like fiction, most humans are aliens not only to themselves but also to the human race. You'll be amazed, that most people do without thinking and that common sense is not as common as the name suggests.

It is the indefiniteness of life that confuses majority of the people and although stupid people can sometimes be positive, man is an unusual collection of inner contradictions.

We all lead double lives like an actor on stage. The lesser roles we play, the better but the more roles we have to play, the more we become less original.

Simply put, there isn't anything in this world as degrading or self destructive or more obscene if we cannot meet up with the demands of life squarely. In order to face life squarely, single bodies must always almost have to stick their neck way out. This way you learn many things, you learn so many useful things without getting hurt, for instance know who you are. The heat you must know is on everybody not just you therefore you have to take off the heat right from inside of you. Find peace and stop hating yourself stop hating people who hate you. We do not have a worldly problem what we have is people to people, nation-to-nation problems.

Were it not for the presence of the unwashed, unclean and its half educated formless queers, politics, incomplete and unreasonable absurd and delightful human animals, the world will be a better place to live in.

There are some frigid souls who think and believe the world as evil, afraid of life, not realizing that the world is harmless if you understand her. We should be working on those people softening them up, enlarging their consciousness and our own too in the process not fighting each other.

Although, I can disagree and agree with doctrines and dogmas, I may not decide to celebrate them.

Amazing world that we are, the further you can extend your chain of alternatives, the less intellect you have but the more positive a choice you can make, the more you can progress in this life.

Crude realism sometimes sounds this way some people are thick, some are blind and most have a faulty wonderful faculty of not seeing and not understanding and are not doing anything about it. So, we send the wrong man to go and see the wrong man. It is a case of the blind leading the blind the two shall fall inside a ditch.

KNOWING YOURSELF

When we are born into this life, it is said that our minds is in a clean state called taburassa that is we know nothing.

As we continue to live, we start to gain experiences and learn from past mistakes to live in the future. There are so many things that the man is made of but distractions in the world make him to pursue a life of vanity instead of realizing his true purpose in life.

Man has been endowed with a lot of instruments to make his living worth while. He has a brain to think eyes to see, nose to smell, ears to hear, legs to walk from place to place, a tongue to taste, hands to feel and a heart to love.

But there is misdirection in man on earth that makes him forget about his normal course and indulges in material pleasures (money, pleasure sex, grand things and women). There are so many sociological, political and mental problems facing man but if man only knows that knowing himself first would be the greatest attribute to conquering all fears.

HOW DO WE KNOW OURSELVES

Man is a conditional being. He is a conditional being in the sense that we are intellectuals, we can think but majority of men have refused to sit down and think. They are too busy with the opus pocus of life. Chasing after the wind, and what do they get worries, mishaps and disasters.

Man's purpose on earth is to study and progress, life on earth is but an illusion it is like a dream, today we are here tomorrow we are gone and no one knows where.

What people have failed to learn is that life gives us exactly what we desire from it. If trouble avoids a person or he avoids trouble, he may become complacement and never have any experience, mans happiness can only come when his heart is free from spite and envy.

Most people spend their time on anxiety and unrest running after worthless and vain things forgetting that experience is the best teacher. Our ideas are our vast empires where we can live happily in our lifetime.

All life is mystery, everyone is a sun and the most powerful man on earth is the one who has himself in the bosom of his own power. If we tend to realize ourselves, it is important to have the right kind of ideas in our minds that is whatsoever things that are true, whatsoever things that are honest, whatsoever things that are lovely, whatsoever things that are pure and of good report, if there be any virtue and if there be any praise give thanks to God. Everybody attracts every other body with a certain force; life is not just a purse for prayers to draw treasures, courage, strength and faith from.

Man himself is the only person who can make himself a slave in his own soul. Perseverance is the only key to will power to developing the inner strength and confidence that can overcome all opposition in a crisis; it is those with will power who survive.

That we should be good and will good for everyone is a concept just as radical today as it was when life began.

Life on earth is a testing place, being yourself the example do only good and no harm to others. Know thyself!

The prosperity of the generous man never fails.

The miser can never find any comforter.

Let the powerful man be generous to the suppliant.

Let him look down the long path of lives, for riches revolve like the wheels of a cart.

They come to one now and then to another.

The beggar today may become a rich man tomorrow.

There are too many strong and wrong notions to achieving our aims that always make some people to fail.

Your life is what you think of it.

LAWS OF LIFE

1. Have faith in everything you do.

2. Study hard

3. Pay honor to your parents including GOD

4. Respect the virtuous

5. Honor elders

6. Help one another

7. Be honest and truthful on all things honesty is money

8. Pay no heed to what friends or relatives talk about you

9. Make the best use of food and wealth

10. Follow only the examples of those who are good.

11. Show gratitude and return kindness for kindness

12. Treat all things with equal measure of goodness

13. Be free from jealousy and envy

14. Refrain from scandal and greed

15. Be gentle in speech, action and harm no one

16. Bear suffering and distress with patience and meekness

17. Being you the example, do good all of the time.

18. God forgives us when we do wrong so let's forgive each other too

19. Being straight with people is what counts in this life; let your spade always be your spade.

It is what the bird eats that it will fly with. Do not ever in your life try to control your life. If you do, you will find out that it is far, far greater than what you think. It will make you fall it will beat you, it will be hard on you but don't control it, Live it live it. If you do not have foresight, you can never see the other side of the mirror.

The world though may be cold when you're on your own just Live it live it. One hand doesn't wash it greases the other. Make no permanent alliances with anybody. Take opponents and challenges and challengers with supreme self-confidence and you will be above the law of suffering. Be self content at all times. Always pride yourself a good loser with a sense of humor.

I regard enormity the way I regard food, a necessity but uninteresting and unimportant.

The body cannot live without the mind. Any road you know in reaching GOD follow it.

Some people are so obsessed with life that they want to carry it on their heads, chest and back until if fell from their hands and broke to a zillion pieces.

Man is an unreal abstraction. I may be a rat but a rat has its pride too and as the past will never be repeated it will never be known and it is best to forget it and live for the future.

The man who does not make mistakes does not usually make anything.

What tears your heart has torn the hearts of many before you and will tear them again and again, age after age. Your wound will heal but it will leave a scar but it will heal. Life is more than meat and the body more than raiment. Evil cannot ever perform well but can come in the disguise of an angel of light.

One who conquers others is great! But one who conquers himself is mighty. There is a difference between knowing the path and walking it. To deny our impulses is to deny everything that makes you human.

Words wound but as a veteran God's Own Child (GOC) you can happily attest to it that words don't kill. Everything in life has a purpose. Life and death has a purpose. You have a purpose. So live the life and discover your purpose in life. Most people live by need and not by truth. If there is a reason for being alive there must be a reason to die.

Do you know the fish? When they're small, they live by the seaside waiting to grow up before they can go deep sea to participate and partake in survival of the fittest but you, you're not even a fish yet you're and egg waiting to hatch. So what is it with you that you carry the entire world on your head?

Tous Passe la vie est continue

Sometimes we are successful sometimes we fail. The strategy is No matter what you do; work always with a clear conscience.

Stop spending your life on anxiety and unrest. Even filthy beggars have guardian angels protecting them. Get past the, what am I getting myself into stage and reach the GOD I'm glad I'm in it level.

SEARCHING FOR WISDOM

WHAT IS WEALTH

Crucial in most fortunes great and small is luck and chance the beneficiary like a raffle winner was at the right place at the right time; people hardly know the meaning of wealth.

They measure wealth in terms of money.

Give man an option of wisdom and money, they will choose money and tomorrow when the money is gone; they will wail and cry and gnash their teeth.

The good news is most people seem to believe in GOD. The bad news is the good news may turn out to be wrong by all that you see and see not you will believe little and understand little but when bad things befall man they become grudgeful and fretful.

Ask! What luck has to do with anything that happens to a man?

Most humans are aliens not only to themselves but to the complicated environment that we live in. we all are creatures of habit and like most creatures of habit, we hate to have plans changed forgetting that it may not be the way we like that we will live our lives.

When one picks himself up and places himself gently into another humans' hands trustingly, the person has immediately began the process of losing especially when you have no business putting yourself in that persons hands even though you were invited.

Why? People struggle in the toils of doubt. They do not know what life is. The confrontation scene, life meets you virtue vanquishes vice. People are thick some are blind and some have a wonderful faculty of seeing and understanding but do nothing about it.

Most people understand where they are but not why. It is the indefiniteness of life that confuses people. There are several people mixed up inside one. It is a double exposure sort of thing there is the warm man and the cold one the cold man gets you into trouble while the warm man gets you out of it people always think life to be a messy business.

The people most likely to be among the early innovators are those who have successfully exposed themselves to many kinds of changes and many types of learning in their lives to a far degree than those who adopt later but while learning builds up learning, learning can also interfere with learning. It can actually make us forget.

All things we may wish to do can never be completed in a lifetime so we are saved by hope. Nothing true or beautiful makes complete sense so we are saved by faith.

Nothing we do no matter how virtuous can be accomplished alone so we are saved by love.

No religion is more powerful than our own spirit and determination if you are defeated in the mind, you are defeated everywhere.

Wealth simply put, is using all the skills you have mastered in life to make a better living in life, you need something you get it then you are wealthy and this brings us to the question of wisdom.

THE JOURNEY OF NO RETURN

<u>WISDOM</u>

What is wisdom?

The only consciousness which one has direct and immediate knowledge of is ones own. One knows the consciousness of others only indirectly. Other beings can never be the object of others perception or experience.

God is wisdom; the spirit of wisdom is intelligence and holiness. It penetrates every spirit that is intelligent and pure. For to the man who pleases GOD, GOD gives wisdom and knowledge and joy but to the sinner, HE gives the work of gathering and heaping only to give to the one who pleases GOD.

Wisdom simply put, begin with the fear of GOD, wisdom moves freely than motion itself; wisdom is a breath of God's power, a pure and radiant stream of glory from the Almighty which is a reflection of eternal life.

Wisdom looks for those who are worthy of her if you do not look for her she will look for you because you are worthy of her.

Wisdom is doing what you're good at and staying away from what you're not good at. It is only the bad people who never think well instead of looking at the flower, the beautiful flower, they look at the thorns. He who suffers much in this world, it is the life that supports him as he is not a master of his life.

Food for the body is food for the heart.

Knowledge drives away ignorance, whosoever that does not know the meaning of what he or she reads or says is an ignorant person insofar as what he or she says or read is pointing to him or her.

GOD will never destroy the world to create another Adam and Eve.

Faith and hope are the finest and the greatest of all spiritual gifts that work together to free a man who has them from being in bondage of power and the dead hand of the past to open for new possibilities of the divine. Genius is simply a by-product of hard concentrated work.

When one produces an unduly complicated solution to a problem, he does not have a solution but has created a new problem.

The prime obstacle to progress is the accommodation of the poor to their plight that is refusal to struggle against the impossible. They accept their poverty what can you get without stretching a little of your neck. You must ever expect to put in something to get or gain something. Better to lose with a wise man than win with a fool.

Most people believe that the bunch of the money is the master key to their whole problem, to them, anywhere you go the road is opened. It is not money that matters but wisdom, with wisdom, you gain everything.

Most people believe that getting money is harder than spending it. Spending money is much, much harder than getting it. Money is just a tool to work with. Money is paper, if you know how to do paper work, you will get money.

It is wisdom that teaches you how to double the money you have without losing it to money doublers. Money is a pussycat! once you understand it and know what you want it to do for you, it is orderly and predictable.

Naturally there is financial reward for all superior intelligence right and wrong are the rules we make up for ourselves because the rules are artificial.

Neither the deer on the hilltop nor the man on the battlefield ever hears the shot that kill them. Wasted space is wasted money wasted time is wasted energy.

THE BIBLE

From Genesis to Revelation, all the writers of the bible all have one thing in common, to do good and worship one true GOD.

Let us assume like majority will assume that the bible is just an historical book. From participating in life we ourselves can see that likes attracts likes what we sow is always what we reap the Bible is a manual for man to live life successfully.

All the prophets in the bible all write about loving one another and we know this is to be true because if we do unto others, as we want others to do unto us we will not have problems.

As for worshipping a GOD we cannot see. All of us at certain intervals will surely know that there is a force for our existence, for how can we come into this world, grow up, make money and die off, there must be a reason.

The bible tells of faith as the substance of things hoped for the evidence of the unseen. Truly if we have faith in GOD, we will always get what we need, it has happened to me and I know it happens to a lot of people.

Therefore, we all have a reason and purpose to be here on earth. I do not have to go into mysticism or psychics but I want to tell you that there are two circumstances in the life of every man, the Controlled and uncontrolled circumstances.

In each we have the power to control one and no power to control the other. If we still take the story of Jesus Christ as a biblical story, we can all see a very good man in him who spoke his mind and thought that the best thing to do in this life is to be good.

He "I am the way" a lot of people are misled by this word Jesus Christ is telling people that they should behave the way he has come to show us to see salvation. But a lot of people believe that he has died for their sins and so they can continue with sin, Jesus Christ is the way by which anybody who goes through him will not perish but have everlasting life.

Majority of people do not know what they need, like or dislike and what they will benefit from or not so they worship money and think money will buy them all things. They developed a culture where everything is measured with money. Religions have been messed up and people work like crazy to impress others. Everything in life has a purpose if there is a reason to be alive there must be a reason to die.

I have not been abandoned by you oh GOD.

I have no friends, no kinsmen but you oh GOD are enough for me. For there is none else like you for my surfeit of joy. For GOD is my life and always gives me my bread of life and leads me always to my source of living waters. The body can never live without the mind. The only way to GOD is to be good. There are many religions, religions of the world are the easiest way to be led astray but one can know the true religion, the religion that preaches goodness of GOD and oneness of man and people doing unto themselves the way they do to others.

Failures are divided into two sub classes, those who thought and never did and those who did and never thought. Being you, the example do only good and no harm to others. Leaders of most religion will tell you the creator has a name. It is only GOD that has the real solutions I will send my special prayer and personally pray for you, tell me your problems, your needs send me your money and so on and so forth.

Idiots will send the money and still want the name of GOD, everyman is an Island no man is father off from GOD than the other. Every man is a GOD created in the image of the almighty creator. To what petty stupidity man will stoop in times of needs.

What I am teaching you is to accept full responsibility of your life by behaving like Jesus Christ, call upon him for all letters of authority as regards living and all your problems will be solved. There is no magic in life. It is just ordinary laws of nature that is GOD.

Man is a spirit, creature of another world and once he can become free of the bounds of the flesh, he can roam the world as a spirit and help others by their thoughts. Death is birth, dying is merely the act of being born again in another place. Man or the spirit of man is eternal; the body is but a temporary garment that houses/clothes the spirit. People who have served their time in hell will be bound to go to heaven.

Although, there are some people in this world who can only grow and develop in the company of others these people should still strive to have time for themselves to remember their almighty creator.

The prosperity of a fool always fails with time. It is the people of the world that cause the life long problems; there is no adventure on earth more exciting and interesting as exploring our own minds. The ideas in our minds are vast. All life is a mystery but he is a slave to life, he who will not attempt to penetrate mysteries. Everyman is a sun; all have a time to roost and a dark side that is hidden from other people.

Life is a series of ups and downs out of which life always returns. The most powerful and wealthy man on earth are those who have themselves in the bosom of their own power that a man who falls in love with himself will never have rivals. Love gives itself it costs nothing. Money is just a tool.

I believe in the testimony of myself my past mistakes and correcting them always asking for assistance from GOD. The Lord is my shepherd I have everything I need. GOD has endowed man with everything he needs in the abundance of water the fool is thirsty every man is a wealthy bank of ideas, and from everything he has lost, he will always gain something and for everything we gain the future remains.

When wealth is lost, nothing is lost.

When health is lost no amount of money can buy it back.

When all is lost, the man is dead and when the man is dead all is lost but the future remains.

Everyman should live by example of Jesus Christ, receiving a new truth is adding a new sense. Experience is the name given to past mistakes to which bank we can always go back to, to withdraw a lot of money to spend in the future, the future always holds.

Everyman aspires after something or the other. It may be mental, physical or spiritual gain. It may be to help others or to only help ourselves unfortunately, men are much in a mess of running after vain things that make them to become undirected, confused, selfish and therefore failed in all they aspire or want to be.

Right and wrong are man made percepts what is right in one part of the world may be totally wrong in another.

When we stop craving for something, we cease suffering for that thing and it comes to us at last if we can just believe. Even the hunters have their lucky day. Receiving a new truth is adding a new sense; people should make do with what they have at hand because life is a tricky business.

Money buys a man the food he eats, the clothes he wears, care when sick, a roof over his head, education, recreation without money he can not even die properly, without money a man cannot die with decency but all these are material things and it is only on the materials scale of preferences that money is most important.

This is a bleak stark cold way of life, no adventure no excitement, no problem, no crisis our philosophy of money should be like that of a man who's never wanted for money. Never spend what you do not have. With the gratification of desires we cannot move forward in the spiritual realm but we will live on the material plane as a selfish and uncontained individual, but with the gratification of our spiritual we can move in the physical and materials plane and be contended always getting what we need at the right time.

This is not a question of belief it is a fact.

When we enjoy something much in August, we always pay back in December and in the hard way, so when adversity befalls let us be contended and know that while we were enjoying some were suffering.

So when tables turn again, when we suffer, let us learn from past mistakes we should take it whole-heartedly.

Tough times never last so when you realize the truth, the sooner you'll ease up and live life and live it well.

MASTERING THE ART OF LIVING

Life is in such a natural state and this confuses people a lot and as most people have forgotten to live we need to help them out a little. Learning to master life is the most valuable tool; it is like mastering a computer. one can develop rather than settling down and folding our arms. Life is simple to understand once you know that everything was created for something. The smallest mosquito has its own purpose.

It requires no special power to understand life if you cannot, you should fall back to the bible for all assistance because in Ecclesiastes 1$^{vs\ 8-11}$, you will find what you need to assist you in the living. "Look! This is something new" it was here already, long ago it was here before our time".

So it is not new and has been here let us learn from that old thing to create a newer and better version. Most men abuse themselves.

Unity of the people can solve all the life long problems if people can unite and act as one loving each other helping each other, there will not be any problems in this life but the reason why this is not so is because of the way some people have developed. Without knowing evil, they can never recognize good. If trouble avoids most people or they avoid trouble for a long time they may become careless and without experience because as we grow we gradually move into the future.

Most people go out to work for money to satisfy their ends and any man who takes up a job for the money it pays has tuned himself into a slave for that job. People prefer to wail and gnash their teeth about what they want instead of doing what had to be done they never seek out opportunities or look within themselves on what they best know how to go about doing it. People go about making complete fools out of themselves. People do not want to take risks as for me, I have gone past he stage of wasting time crying about the way I look or behave in the society, I never get myself into any trouble I cannot get myself out of.

Sun means money everyday above the ground is a good day. If you are short of money, use what you have to get what you need

Try always to turn a disadvantage into an advantage and then you would have conquered your greatest enemy which is yourself.

Study the environment you live in try to go through the environment as if you are invincible that no one sees you so no one can help you. If you loose in something think rise above that pain that has made you fail, digest that pain, why did I fail, look for loop holes why I failed, block them and try again do not ever be afraid of trying again and again. If you are not afraid to look into your fears then you can learn to overcome them without knowing.

Making plans is the greatest thing in one's life, maybe the plans do not work well for the moment maybe something we thought about as right goes wrong at the last moment and our plans disappears like the wind, the fun is in making the plan to look ahead and plan we may not succeed in the planning of everything but we should continue planning. One of them will jell on the long run.

A road is truly two in one to see if you have to see it coming and going so if one plan does not work change the plan but never the goals to which your plan was made to manifest. Always know that we all have our losses and they may cripple us sometimes but what we should learn is from those losses. We should bow down for the inevitable once we know if it's inevitable we should not be crippled and invite leprosy again into our lives.

There will be no problem of money or merchandise miss road if money and merchandise exchange at the right time.

Any thinking that does not satisfy our spiritual hunger to mobilize us fully is destined to fail. Realization does not take place fully unless emotions are deeply involved to make something happen the way we want it we have to think deeply about that thing become one with it, know the loop holes and plug them have faith in it, think it, see it, visualize it then do it.

Forty-five years of my life have been spent in schools. The other years again it's just another kind of school I don't always try to be like the little marrow who hides in his own small eddy of black water not realizing that all the world are his to play in clinging only to one place.

The only thing in life that makes any meaning is GOD with GOD you are somebody with GOD you suddenly become man with GOD you can always know that you have been endowed by nature with a lot of power to preserve your life. Always raise your own life high/higher never let yourself be dropped down this is why those in power in this world are ready to do everything possible even to kill to hold on to that power because power corrupts.

Do not ever be afraid of failing. It has stopped most people from achieving their goals. Man like animals was made to live together with others like himself but the true meaning of belonging to such a group can be found in the comfort of deep thinking.

There will be no more mysteries when one finds GOD in his life. It is always better to be good and live a short life than to be bad and livelong. It is also better to make small and be happy than to make much and die. It is better to make small money with rest of mind than to make much with a lot of problems.

We steal more from ourselves than we steal from other people. Nothing worth ever having is so easy. As a man you must walk through the life of destiny without drinking too much from the cup of vanity because vanity upon vanity all is vanity.

We must not fear because destiny has brought in to life, we must not brood on our past or waste time dreaming into a future that may never be; we should concentrate more on the present what will be must be.

With power of your mind and faith you can move mountains, think relax and stay with faith and impossibilities become possible. With the power of your mind you can beat the unbearable and see into the unseen and will never have fear in coping with life.

This is an evil world. He who can point the way to peace, justice, salvation, everlasting joy and love is a messenger to this life to make it peaceful and he himself will only find happiness.

Our faith not only rescues us from spiritual death but it gives us and serves us greater joy in our present lives. To the man who bows down to GOD there is no limit to his everlasting peace within him.

Be conservative in what you do, be liberal in what you can accept from others. The world is full of godless and wretched men.

If we fall into rubble, we will always come out of the ruins and there comes us again as we can build up once more to watch once more all that we have built fall again. It should be amusing to us because what ever we build we can never take with us when we die so when it falls, we should not kill ourselves; if we do, it is an emotional sickness i.e. you are acting without the benefit of your internal intellect.

If you ever desire to help a friend, do so in such a way that it will never bring that friend's burden upon yourself because it is useless to attempt to reason a man out of what he has never actually reasoned into.

We should live happily while other people spend their lifetime in anxiety and unrest. All that people desire is worthless when we die but that which we will possess if we follow God's plan in abundance because it is certain that we will never fulfill all our hopes and wants in a lifetime but with GOD all our needs will always be fulfilled.

As for time, all men have it in abundance. You and I have two frames of references and never shall they meet but one thing is certain, "GOD loves merciful men".

An example of a greedy man can be likened to the silkworm; the more silk it spins round itself the less of a chance it has of living until it finally dies also Midas also turned everything to gold until he had no food to eat.

THINKING

The way we think affects how we live; the way we perceive ourselves affects our purpose in life because if we do not believe that we can so something, it becomes impossible for us then we would not be able to do it even if we had knowledge to do it. If we create a more positive attitude to our way of thinking, we can greatly improve our self-esteem.

People who are failures in this life affect themselves with thinking that they are failures and so they fail. Everyday man has to face a lot of problem situation but it is a problem because all problems have solutions. If one approaches life with more optimism the person will cope better with stressful conditions and thus be able to calculate and solve problems efficiently.

If one thinks about what one needs and what one wants, if we concentrate on having it, we will get it but if we intentionally block our own desires and prevent our subconscious from getting what we want due to maybe financial constraints then we will not get it.

We should develop a more positive attitude to what we want and think on this line that which we want will eventually come to us.

What we think of yourself and the society we live in creates our reality. Any little thought consciously or unconsciously becomes and intention and if it was meant to fail, it will always fail. People also perceive us the way we perceive ourselves; likes attracts likes when we change our negative self image then we can stop hating ourselves and appreciate whatever we do. Once we do this, others will follow.

A positive self-image builds makes us achieve our goals without us feeling it but because pessimism leads to doubts and doubt makes us fear, fear makes us never to want to try in the first place and not wanting to try leads to failure.

If we can think it then we can do it.

Being positive in the mind makes us the types of person we want to be.

If we motivate ourselves for GOD, GOD will motivate us for success.

Once we replace our negative thoughts with positive ones and with a little prayer, we start to get positive results.

REALISING ONES GOALS

Everything in the world is everybody's. When our vision of GOD gets blurred, frustration sets in the skills we learn on the street and off the street are valuable; the person who can merge the two together quickly is the achiever.

Things we learn in schools only help us to be better in relating to others. It is the things we learn on the street that makes us to be brilliant.

There is always a GOD sent business for the man who wants quietness and ease of mind.

One should wait for his own time. Although people may always think that it may be too late, time is what we have in abundance.

If we have learnt anything in life, it is what we have learnt on the street; if we want to move forward it is what we learnt form the bible, if we want to achieve more from life we should emulate Jesus Christ.

It is not the amount of money that one has that makes him wealthy; it is how good you are living your life. When you need something and you can get it; when you are hungry and you can eat, when you are faced with a cross situation, you can solve it without money and with money you can live.

Then your wealth is enormous all you have to do is wait for the divine intervention to get the real big ideas of yours to become a reality.

Do it yourself if you want it done right.

As one struggles more and more as one seeks to know the truth, the mind attains a higher conscious far greater than those who are immovable. As the mind attains a higher consciousness, truths and understanding of GOD materializes.

All creative thought requires an act of faith, the man must trust his intention, The spontaneous creations of his experience and new knowledge.

One should always narrow and eliminate. It is better to be systematic and careful in the world that we live in.

Fear can prompt all sorts of unusual behaviors and if one tries to get even with the world or someone that has offended us it is a sickness and weakness of the mind we wear, whosoever we are inwardly and outwardly as life is a series of games One after another. Death is another and greatest of all games that you find out the result only when you are dead.

I am yet to see one who died and came back to tell us this is what happened. We should always discourage disagreement and urge compromise to move forward and live life. Life is full of secrets and we cannot learn them all in one lifetime. GOD grants us the strength to accept those things we cannot change.

If we allow others to pity us what we should always realize is that it is always the person pitied that is always at the end of the suffering not the person that pity's us.

Your way will always catch up with you as a night full of passion can also give you a lifetime of pain. So in whatsoever we do let us always give a chance to pain and suffering when hey come let us pass through them without suffering and pain.

Although it is general that bad people always make good people bad, we should strive to do good at all times although people tends never to listen to the man of truth except the man who has to lie to them and tell them what they believe in "Bring me your money and I will tell you the name of GOD". Majority of the people are sick.

For any man who has decided to learn, he should be prepared to go round the corner to find the truth. Knowledge does not end in man made schools. Every step we take every move we make, we should be strong and never say "I don't know what to do. As it happens to one so it happens to another".

Those who are prepared to learn the truth should have their eyes, nose and ears opened because you will find out in your time that if you do not give loyalty and friendship, when your time of trouble and difficulties come you will have to bear your cross alone. Loyalty and friendship are thing beyond price.

It is impossible to ever teach another how to use his sense of perception if the person belief system does not acknowledge its existence.

This is always the problem with people. They can't stand up on their own they cannot speak their mind but I suggest that we should never delegate responsibility to another person, you should trust no one. There is no adventure on earth, more exciting like exploring ones own mind but because most people always delegate their thinking to others, they will always be poor. No religion is more powerful than our own spirit and determination.

Heavy the sorrow that bows the head when you are alive and hope is dead remember my people the best people on earth always make themselves. Remember also, if you are defeated in the mind, you are defeated everywhere because your success like failure starts from the mind. If you want it done right, then do it yourself.

The best men always make themselves. With money, without money you should be able to cope with life. Yesterday can be known but tomorrow is impossible.

If anybody tells you they know your tomorrow they are lying. Nobody on earth knows tomorrow. That person you are taking your problem to, to solve for you also has his own problems that he is not able to solve. So it is like the blind leading the blind both shall fall into a ditch.

If you plan and that plan does not work change the plan but never the goal, do not let your fate be like that of Midas who touched everything and they turned to gold till he never had anything to eat can he eat gold when he touches food it turns to gold.

The world is made for black and white times. If there was no evil we will never know that good existed.

Wasted space is wasted money, wasted time is wasted energy, life is like electricity once you know and understand here then you can know what to expect of her. Life is orderly and predictable. What you sow is what you reap.

If you are true to yourself, you can never be false to another. You have to pass through life to receive the grace of God. God does not invite hardship on any man. It is ourselves that bring hardship upon us. No man is farther from God than the other we were all equal before God. So where other people have gone short and not achieve their goals, we should go far and wide to always seek for a solution.

If the truth does not come to us we seek the truth. Everybody's doing makes him what he/she is in this world sometimes when dreams come true they die.   No matter what we should understand that we are always falling and falling out of the hands of God. Falling, falling and falling only to be caught up again in the hand of GOD. Do not ever underestimate the power of human stupidity. We all are created to participate in a role in this life and unless we realize that role, we can never be happy but once the role is participated in happiness comes our way as our needs will always be fulfilled by using our reasoning in GOD.   A mans happiness comes only when his heart is free from spite and envy.   Truth is always simple.

Never appeal to another mans better nature he may not understand you as he may not have one become through violence you may murder the liar but you cannot murder the lie nor at the same time be able to establish the truth. Do not be like those that wish kindness but who they themselves are incapable of showing kindness.

Life will not be sacred unless it has a purpose and meaning and in placed and enjoyable without controversy there can be no wise argument without dissention there can be no agreement without disaster there can be no peace what crimes have been committed in this world in the name of conscience. A man can never trust his conscience unless it is in perfect accord with God.

When a man's testes withers, his wisdom flowers each man has his season in this life. People kill one another because they want the other to believe in what they believe what a world if as individuals we do not reach the stage of knowing ourselves and accept ourselves we cannot and ever be in comfort in this life we should grow to know and understand GOD as there is no profit in wickedness.

The GOOD LORD GOD will never suffer the soul of the righteous to famish. So, sow the good seed into your mind while others plant evil when the harvest comes, what you sow is what you reap.

Try to understand people's actions for this; you have to know his to understand how he thinks today, you have to know how he thought yesterday. Only past and present will let the truth out. If you look to others for what to do, you will never make a difference in this life, you are a vault of ideas all you have to do is to tap into your subconscious and with little prayers you will succeed. Always know that because you have a past, you can calculate or know your future. If your past is bad you can change the future for good.

I have known some people for some years as they were growing up they were not scoundrels but recently they became one with years of living and trying to cope with life. Most people have undergone such great and dramatic changes besides; some have become swindlers as well. People who do not do what they enjoy are never happy.

Do not ever fear fear, fear is just an uncontrolled imagination acting against the will. Life is like a chess game. Players playing for the same price "HEAVEN and ETERNAL LIFE" but everybody are uneasy about how it will end.

There is no magic involved in life it is all ordinary laws of nature that GOD put for us.

The man who makes no mistakes does not usually make anything.

Devotion is very moving but you must never allow it to becloud you from the truth. If you are dependent on men to do your thinking for you, you will always be poor. We should not be chasing our problems, we should be solving them.

Men growing old will find out that substitute experience and cunning for genius. They scavenge ideas to put bits and pieces together from their long chain of experience they have had. There are some things worth   laughing about when you cannot really do anything about them. When it is good it is good and vice versa.

If the approach to life is more of a cheerful way, we can always cope better in problems, situations and solve them more efficiently as they come.

If one wants to attract financial abundance it is always better to think in the times of what you want to always develop a more positive attitude towards the goal.

ATTRACTING FINANCIAL ABUNDANCE

By creating positive thinking, one can greatly increase financial abundance because having a positive mental attitude attracts positive effects in ones life.

When one replaces negative thoughts and beliefs with positive thinking then one can move forward on the ladder to financial abundance.

You can get it if you really want but you must try. Any man who spends all his time with his family and never has more time to study himself can just become a slave to his work if he has one.

If one has a goal to be achieved one should always find time alone to delve and think upon ways to achieve that goal. It is always better sometimes to write all the positive ways of achieving that goal down and then narrow them down to the most profitable condition of achieving them. Whatsoever we think of the world and ourselves invariably, intentionally and unintentionally block our desires to achieving those goals when we think negatively and may thus prevent us from achieving that goal. Also the way we think affects our health too. In the sense that if we always think negative, they drain us of substantial energy that could have been used in thinking well.

Being positive changes our behavior and never wants us to do bad because if one is positive he will know those things which are good smile a lot and be happy at all times because he will know as it happened to the rich man so it happens to the poor man both are under the sentence of death.

If one is downcast, he should motivate himself to do something he loves doing, it may be to talk to others about goodness, it may be to want to change other for good at the end of the pouring out your mind, you would have exhausted yourself of all negative thinking preparing yourself for the positive thinking which worldly distractions might have caused.

One should be focused by being focused does not necessarily mean that one should become a one way track minded person but one should be able to discard and accept all possibilities and negativities and do away with those things that will hinder him from being financially abundant. Waste is one of the things we should always learn to do away with.

Do not even waste water; try to be conservative try to be content with whatever you have at any point in time and always know that if one road is blocked another will open.

One should refrain from too much talking as too much talking draws the body of enough energy that could be used in running a 400metres race.

In the process of attracting abundance, higher self esteem, better health, motivation, attracting conducive circumstances, total relaxation are some of the tools one has to work with, let us now discard them one by one.

BETTER HEALTH

When we send the rainmaker to explain how bread is made to the bread maker, we ourselves know we have error. For example if one wants to be rich, will he go and stay with the poor definitely, if he stays with the poor he will sooner or later starts to think like the poor at the end of the day.

Mental, physical and spiritual health is highly essential in attracting financial abundance. If one is mentally sick (and a lot of people are) it becomes more difficult to achieving aims and goals when one is sick and goes to the hospital, the doctors cure that sickness but not the cause of the illness. So what happens when we get sick again of that same illness and so it goes round and round.

If we are sick, we should not only cure the sickness but also abstain from the cause of it then it will be fully eradicated.

Our philosophy of better health includes not only thinking about financial abundance, love wealth work but thinking deeply about ourselves and what brings us to discomfort. A lot of people forget themselves in the process of living that when they break down they now run to a doctor for remedy and treatment of that illness but never the cause.

A lot of people are sick and in pain not only of living, but of far greater mind disease than they phantom.

People have forgotten that their bodies are the temple of GOD and that it must be kept clean. They defile the body and then run to a hospital or doctor for remedy. Thoughts, actions and emotions affect greatly our mental health.

Our thoughts and actions coupled with our intentions and imaginations creates visualizations which when they are genuine and directed only towards genuine needs as most people bring harm to others through greed, if we can direct our thoughts only for good then only good will flood our way as our needs and desires will be achieved through a divine intervention.

DIVINE INTERVENTION

When all roads seems blocked when we look to the right, left front and back and it seems there is no person to turn to when we think that all is lost at this time with just a little prayer, divine intervention is on the way because of this time our thought are greatly directed towards achieving our goals thus we have replaced unconsciously negative thoughts and belief system with positive thinking in fact it is only at times like this that experience is always put to play because we become more daring in our desires and we know we have all the knowledge, skills and know of what we need at that particular time.

We become one with the problems in our dreams because of the seriousness of the calamity we are in and if we think deeply that why? Why? I am capable of accomplishing this feat, then the thing we so desire manifests and we get it then we are happy.

Divine intervention works for all of us all the time, it is a way GOD uses to bring us back to His reality but what usually happens is that immediately we are relieved of our burdens by divine intervention a lot of people refuse to learn and always go back to the shit that put them in that condition in the first place.

But if we are the thinking types we will makes sure that situation never repeats itself thus we learn and move forward.

This once we have achieved a goal that seemed impossible our stress is diminished and this can lead us to finishing other projects that we have planned.

In order to get rids of the past situation we have to plan for the future because as all of us have a past we can always use the past to predict the future if we are the thinking and learning type. The funniest thing about life is that people use the wrong approach to facing life. The only reason why we face problems and dilemmas is because we put them ourselves, we invite them into our lives it is only the person that allows his problems to override him is the loser.

The problems we created and the solution to it is what the man needs for him to move forward.

I am yet to see the man who died and came back to the world to world to tell us what to expect when we die from here, once we know that there are certain things we can never know the more we will settle down and live a peaceful life.

A lot of people are too carried away by focusing their lives on goals, relationship, finances, career or achievements forgetting that we are what we are and our bodies is the only true shelter that we have our bodies lies all the solutions to our basic problems.

Our bodies is a huge mechanism by which if one part is faulty all other parts will not function properly thus we can raise or diminish our body functions by the way we think or relate to others.

No food on earth is as sweet as knowing who we really are and knowing how to attract goodness and repel evil. In whatever we do, there is always a break thus into whatever we cease to expect.

Our lives are crystal clear just like nature everything works for everything. Man work for his guard him from certain dangers, he feeds the dog for the dog to bark well when intruders approach, this are all the nature of life that we live in, everything works for everything, without everything working for everything, the world would not have a meaning. The smallest mosquitoes have what they do in life. If they were to be eradicated, they will leave their toll on life.

All extinct animals have served their purpose on earth so they are no more. If and when two would have finished his purpose on earth he will die.

No man can ever die before his time for it is appointed unto each man the time of death. When people talk about untimely death, I always laugh because my belief system does not believe in what they call untimely.

Every man on earth has a purpose when he out uses his purpose he retires and dies for other people to come into the life and keep on her existence adding their own quota to her. Life is endless; it is only the man whose time has come that his life ends.

Who knows maybe it is even after life that the life begins to be better, who knows it may even be that the life is a school preparing us for higher lives who knows after death.

A lot of people talk of life after death, how many of these people have partake in the life after death, everybody is guessing. Nobody knows.

This is also why everybody's life is different from others; father's life is different from son or daughter, brothers differ from each other, classmates sometimes share common interests' strangers too. This is why we just like another more than the other and are attracted to others more than others.

Everybody has a specific goal and sometimes the way we think we will achieve our goals may not be the way nature "GOD" planned for us, so what do we get? We start walking round in circles never making headway. Divine intervention tries to straighten us when we loose too much track; she puts us in the right way yet again and again a lot of people still derail.

The art of trying to master life with the wrong approach is the cause of life long problems and suffering of majority because when we tackle a problem with the wrong solution, we do not solve the problem but have created a new problem then we get sick. Simple truth will always save us from a lot of sickness, fatigue and pain.

If the type of environment we create for ourselves makes it difficult for us to function properly. Environment here does not reflect on the society but on our own mutual actualization that is if we keep too much trash on feed too much trash into our subconscious then the ability to function well will be hindered.

The body can be described as a machine for it to function well, other parts must work together for the benefit of other parts then the fuel our blood if it is nourished well regarding what we eat, how much sleep we get, thinking well not being greedy or not self sufficient than a lot of illness sets in frustration stress. Madness, foolishness, ungratefulness, stinginess and so on disrupt our way of life, which has been mapped out for us.

Life is like a jigsaw puzzle you have to find the parts to make the puzzle real but in the process of making the jigsaw puzzle become whole. A lot of people miss the road; the life can also be compared to a typewriter whereby you press the wrong buttons and you get terrible answers that you yourself may not even be able to pronounce.

Our life that is the fuel that makes us tick, our blood must be kept nourished at all times then with a little bit of prayer all things comes our way because our bodies was created to balance all things we do and this is why people usually say that too much of everything is bad. Too much of greed, poverty, money, water, everything is bad. We have to check balance what we do eat, see and think in our subconscious because our subconscious stores all the information we come across getting us ready to plunge into the future.

A man without a past can never make anything in the future because it is the past that dictates what happens to us next. The past is there for us always to tap into and for us to make corrections and this helps us to move forward while divine intervention corrects us more when we are led astray totally.

THE LORD IS MY CONFIDENCE
KNOWLEDGE CALLED WISDOM

Happy is the man that findeth wisdom.

The LORD by wisdom created the earth and established the heavens.

We should never be afraid of sudden fear or desolation or distractions of the wicked when they come, we should never withhold good to whom it is due both animal and man we should never device evil against our neighbors we should try never to strive with man without cause, we should keep God's words alive and bind his words upon our hearts, we should call unto wisdom as a sister and call understanding our kin man. Wisdom is better than all the money in the world put together. Wisdom is a sound mind full of understanding and strength. Riches, honor and happiness are with wisdom.

Blessed is the man that listens to GOD for whoso findeth GOD findeth understanding and happiness, whoso is simply at heart will find GOD and wisdom and understanding, whoso findeth wisdom will eat of her bread and drink of her wine. People should try to forsake the foolish ways and go in the way of understanding.

The fear of the LORD is the beginning of wisdom. The knowledge of the HOLY Spirit is understanding.

WORK YOURSELF TO GET WHAT YOU NEED
USING TOO MUCH TIME TO FIND LESS MONEY
USING MONEY TO FIND MONEY

USING OTHER PEOPLE'S MONEY

A lot of people work because they think that their job will get them what they want, it is only when they start the job that they find out that before the end of the month, before being paid their salaries, they have spent more than half of it on credit, transport etc. Then the plan "A" let me just work for a few months and save enough money to start my life becomes let me work for few more years and see if I will still be able to save enough money as the years go by, the rules pertaining to the work remains the same everyday becomes tomorrow and tomorrow and becomes next year. The man starts to look for promotion, to get the promotion; he has to be extremely good at his job. The man has made himself a slave to his job. There is no going back now, he has to work and be of good behavior to become a pensioner. He has already six children. His initial plans have gone posh but who knows, one of his six children may become the president tomorrow so he pours all his income on the children. This is in case of a good father.

The action of working for some time before moving forward has caused him to move backward in life and remain redundant in one spot for life. The problems of majority of men is that they think they are to preoccupied with doing what they think they will benefit from they have forgotten that everyday something is done, the same way for years, monotony sets in. if most men are doing the jobs they hate most in life, they want to put on ties drive cars and have no rest of mind.

They have failed to realize that it is better to do something for nothing than doing nothing at all i.e. if nothing is done, we have left nothing undone.

Too many people are too obsessed with doing than setting plans. People have been conditioned from birth to do things because other people are doing it and thus reverse are always the case to moving forward.

Things have to get really hard to allow a man to focus on what one desires but fear, anxiety, doubt and worries of hunger, clothing, meeting up with peer group have stopped most people from achieving their aims than I care to think about.

If one can work himself to the stage of focusing a desire and not do anything until he has visualized his desires then he or she can make that desire real in the subconscious and the mind will lead the person on the next line of action.

Imagination plays a greater role in our achievements than going to school; knowledge only helps us to calculate better.

The best things in life are free if you know how to get it. Everyone of us have been programmed to get what we want but the approach most people have in getting what they think they need or want is wrong. There is a difference in what we need and what we think we need.

We may not need a car and think we need it because most of our friends have cars and if it is not raising status in the society, so we go and buy a car. We have failed in so many aspects.

We have forgotten that the car has to move, repair tires, the unforeseen accidents etc. they all cost more money. This is wrong judgment to our needs and thus what we thought would satisfy our needs in the first place has become another problem in our lives.

Why! We could have first used the money we used in buying the car for a business that will yield us profit at the end of the day. It may be two years, three years then we have enough profit to assist us in buying a car that can now assist us in the business we are doing.

But reverse is always the thinking of men. If you are not showing off that you are better off than the next man then we think we are not moving forward.

Do you know how many spend so much on accommodation but cannot feed well at home?

In some societies, your dressing tells people who you are but do you know how many wear good clothes carry the best bags but do not have an office.

Life is not by all the work, we can do, people work themselves into frenzy the people who work the hardest always make the least. All work and no play make Jack a stupid man.

Too much repetition and too much hard work kills the brain for future better development of the inner self. All the people I have known who work a lot never think well until they are maimed from the job or were retired all of a sudden sometimes due to bad health and without fringe benefits.

These people have hurt themselves in the struggle for life. The fact of life is that the more one struggles to please others, the more his magnetic force of attraction is directed towards opposite directions to which one may never have desired.

If we read our bible, we can see the ease to which GOD had created the earth all from the words of mouth "Let there be" "and there was". The less we do things with force or do things by need then we can live a little happy. Most of our actions are borne out of fear of failure but we should know that GOD never created any man to fail.

If we analyze even how our body functions we will see that everything regenerates if proper care of it is taken.

It is the misinterpretation of life that carries majority out of the way of their goals. Thus when we force any desire to manifest through a particular action we may fail or harm our thinking and ourselves.

Everything works for everything for every little action there is a reaction, if we can think then we will eat, have things we desire and there will be less suffering. It is never our actions that make anything to happen in our lives rather most actions lead to distractions and distractions leads to frustrations and frustrations leads to being sick in the head and this leads to being sick in the mind and when we are sick in the mind nothing can be achieved.

Always remember that no man has any control over his life and if you do not have control over certain issues in your life, you should let those things you can never change be.

There is no secret to living as it comes be content with her, come rain come sunshine become one with yourself be cool and calm always facing all situations with less anxiety until your time is up then you can say I did my best.

If you always have or make a decision to copy others or listening to what others feels about you then you are in the process of loosing your track of time and who you are

It is only dead people that people do not gossip about. Listening to other peoples opinion of yourself is bad know that blood flows in all of us all for the same purpose but way our body functions is totally different from each other.

This is why some people can drink ten bottles of beer and still be sane and another will drink half a glass of beer and become insane. Our body functions are the same; all working towards the same goals but how they will work towards the same goal is what is different from individual to individual.

You have to pass through the life for the life to pass through you, if you hinder passing through life, you have hindered life passing through you. There is checks and balances in all that we do, what is good for Mr. 'A' may not be acceptable to Mr. 'B' or harmful to him but all of us are working towards the same goal to make the life better and a better place to be (a paradise) with love abundance and light giving us all enough energy to survive.

Make your life real in your mind and doors you never expected will open without keys and effortlessly then the life herself will help you to get what you need from her but if we do otherwise, then the universe will provide us a different view to the set of circumstances that may befall us, how we behave attracts what we need, if we behave bad, bad will never finish from our house, if we do good, good will always trail us.

We should forget the old notion that all great wealth was passed down through inheritance. I have seen a slave become king and a king become prisoner whatsoever you gave to life; life will give back to you. I am yet to see any man or magician who will plant corn and reap apples. Whatever you sow in you is what you reap outside. Life is a continuous ball game of doing good and running away from things that are bad.

The LORD is everyman's shepherd HE has given us everything we need but a lot of people are misled thinking that GOD settles his accounts on the 30th of each month or yearly. All people I have known insisted on living a bad life or wicked life always ended up badly sooner or later, the bad life catches up with them unaware.

CONDITIONALITY POWER IN US

What we should all know in this world is that we are all co-creators in this universe. Like I always say everything works foe everything hatred works for good and vice versa. In regards to wealth, if we look back to our past we will know that life is a collection of past experiences.

Let us look back at times when we needed money sometimes it looks like we were finished and there was nothing to make us go right again. Sometimes we were so broke that the life was not worth living without money, then all of a sudden out of nowhere our thinking faculty whispers to us we listen because there was nothing to listen to and money comes out, then we laugh and are happy again forgetting our past problems.

If at this stage we continued to listen to that whisper in our minds we would have continued to get money but immediately the money gets into our hands enjoyment and all those things we missed when we did not have money erode our thoughts the we spend the money lavishly on cars good and expensive wine, women, jewelries etc the money finish we go back to square one.

Men who make most of money and become wealthy are those people who make money first work for them then later they can reap all the enjoyments they did not have when they now have abundance.

Most people in this world keep an amazing wealth and never have time to enjoy the wealth they are preoccupied with gathering and gathering until they died in the process.

This is why most wealth that is enjoyed is from inheritances. The man who amassed the wealth did not enjoy it, he leaves it for the one who has not worked for it and this man enjoys it.

If at all times we look at the experience we often find ourselves, if it is that of not having money, then something is wrong somewhere and it is so simple but a lot of people may not realize it.

We may be radiating negative thoughts in our doings and subconscious. There is enough million out here to satisfy everybody and when I hear people say I do not think I can make it, I laugh and tell them you can make it. People doubt their capabilities not realizing that they are part of co-creating the world.

If there is any doubt in our minds, then we can not be in control of the creation we were meant for. If only we can create our own experiences with our minds then we can be rich because all like force starts from our minds.

People unconsciously destroy their own efforts when it comes to their being successful; sometimes people take one step forward and ten steps backward only to learn all over and over again.

COMMUNICATION WITH NATURE

The bible says, "Ask and you shall be given,

Seek and you shall find

Knock and the door shall be opened.

What most people have failed to see is that those things they fear and worry about always happens. So that means we have thought about the fear and it materializes.

If we change these thoughts and focus then highly on things we want they also will materialize. Thus if we ask and ask we get that which we ask for, if we ask for bad, we get bad; if we ask for good, we get good. If we communicate with the universe, the universe has all the answers for us but we need to be careful in our communication because if it is for bad intention then we may invite calamity but if it is of good intentions then we laugh, if we observe our lives we will find out that things come to us in ways we never planned and sometimes they give credence much better to that which we had planned of hoped for.

If we think and desire to succeed for a time we will succeed because a goal set with certainty is already accomplished.

So if we want to do something that we know, we do that, that we know and leave that which we do not know because it can never be known and that we do not know will not harm us.

Nature is miraculous, everything does not look the same but all things work for the same purpose to make the life a better place.

The sun rise the sun sets, the rain falls, the air blows, man is born, he grows and dies off and the world remains the same blooming.

A million things go right for us everyday right from the time we were born till the time we die but everyday we unconsciously destroy our own made efforts and success. We hurt ourselves more than we hurt others thus we are our own enemy.

Most people associate money with wealth but this is not so, wealth simply put is happiness. Yes it is being able to get whatever you need at the right time being content and being all able to differentiate between good and evil. The aim of life is to be happy and to enjoy her. It is happiness that we all sought after. Money does not bring happiness it is happiness that brings money most wealthy people never have money in their pockets but can order for anything they wish at the spur of the of the moment.

If one wish for money, he will always work harder and harder to get that money and whatsoever he spends, he will want to work harder to replace. Thus he continues to work harder and harder. No amount of money is ever enough and this is the most difficult thing about making money. Most of us can never make enough and we cannot make enough surplus. Making money in the first instance is easy but spending, it is the more difficult and so when we have spent it while the going is good, then when we become broke again all kinds of challenges face us again and we become lost in the myriads of how to get more money. People have forgotten that if they can find a way to give values to others, the money will follow and happiness is sure.

People run all the places looking for wealth not realizing that they are wealthy.

GLORIFICATION OF GOD

This is where the deepest secret of happiness manifests the concepts of GOD.

To me it is very good, I believe it, and I feel it, I live it, and I enjoy it because at all times it makes me happy. It is food for my thoughts, it let's me know which things I should do, be careful of and never do at all.

It curtails most men from doing evil and makes men live happily towards each other. If most men could adhere to the concept of GOD as I call it, the world will be the best place to live in.

The concept of GOD as I put it is the truth about one that wants to live life. You do not have to be a religious person to believe in the concept of God. You do not even have to belong to any religion; however, we put it, if we know that the sole purpose of man is to worship and sing praises to the most high our problems will be diminished.

To glorify or communicate with higher persons has been age-old history and all kinds of people have been heard to glorify GOD in times of need.

Glorification of GOD brings happiness like I have never known before to me.

All the heights of glorifying I have sometimes felt my spirit yoking with a higher spiritual realm that I cannot explain and I have used glorifying GOD to solve so many problems. Even when I was growing up and did not know many things. I have used glorification of God to solve so many mysteries pass exams get out of troubles, make money, directed wealth to my door steps, and traveled without expectation, traveled without money, healed myself when sick to mention a few.

Glorification of GOD brings happiness to me, I am sure if you glorify GOD too you can share in the bliss that is felt. GOD, is very rich and spiritual, HE loves praises. When we fall into a bad mood, I suggest singing to lift us out if it.

For most of us, the fact is that as humans we have been given everything to make us never to suffer but unconsciously we create our own experiences otherwise if one thought of acquiring millions and sings and sings to himself that he has acquired the millions, the millions comes to him. Spiritual sensations of the songs that we sing in the spiritual realm are so fascinating that to know about it we have to die first.

This is my own theory of why the devil became bad it may not be acceptable to you but from so much reading I came to conclude why he is trying to lead men astray.

"When GOD created the earth devil Satan whatever you choose to call him was given the job of praise singing in heaven. He was the chief enjoyment officer in heaven.

Then GOD said let us create man in our image and give him the job of praise singing". Because GOD formed men out of sand, the devil became very jealous and asked himself why GOD should take away his ministerial post of enjoyment officer and give it to lesser person, someone made from soil, he therefore rebelled and fell short of the glory of GOD, he has entered into men's hearts using the vanities of life to deceive then he has led many astray through violence, greed and blinded majority. Most people have not realized that the attempt to escape from evil thoughts and to do what is good at all times is the only salvation to man.

Like this is the devil or Satan or whatever you call him can never come near you as would have been given the two options of life and you will be able to differentiate between good and evil and good always overrides evil.

When a man moves away from evil, he will not have the problem of temptation that is the devil and when one is tempted you can use glorification to ward away all evil. It is from clapping the hands that leads to dancing.

Glorification simply means singing praises to GOD to attain higher spiritual enlightenment, let us sing praises and when we have been directed away from our problems let us always learn from our past mistakes called EXPERIENCE.

EXPERIENCE

When a man with experience meets another man with money, the man with the experience generally ends up with the money while the man with the money, if he has learn anything ends up with an experience by which he can make more money. That is the money he has lost. Most people never learn from past mistakes and observations, all their thoughts, are constantly being clogged off by all their thoughts of fear and worries and the outcome always leads to miseries.

When an individual is divided within himself, the center can never hold thus much of the sufferings in this world are self-chosen.

Thus when we carry ourselves, and gently place ourselves into another person's hand, we have not solved our problems but have created a new problem for ourselves. The greatest reason why most people worry is because of money and because we can never know the future we can calculate it from the past, which is a collection of past experiences.

All life is a cycle, what you sow is what you reap. If we sit down to observe our past lives we will notice that it is mostly those things we planned for most that takes a lot of time to materialize. If we know this then we should also know that some things can never be changed. So what do we do? We do not know for those who know. Let us never bother ourselves with the things we do not know because no matter how we strive to know, we shall never know and thus we would never solve a lot of problems and time saving.

Our struggling in life is due to our resistance to divine inspiration and intervention in our lives. We always assume that we know all when we actually know nothing.

Man was created to enjoy being a praise singer to the almighty, to come into the world and multiply to sing more and more and enjoy.

Jesus Christ turned water to wine and people drank and were merry. Notice "Merry" ask yourself why did he have to change the water into wine. Wine is an alcoholic beverage and to drink and to drink it to a merry mood, people must have taken cups and cups of it.

Why didn't Jesus Christ leave the water as it is and let people drink water. Yes He wanted the crowd to be happy this is the purpose of GOD in our lives, if we accept him HE created us to live with each other and to be happy always to love one another and to lead one another from evil.

No man was created to suffer but there is too much emphasis on suffering in this life. This is because most people have forsaken the way of the most high and have started seeking their own.

They believe they know everything not realizing that they know nothing. If we create experiences that are good, they will motivate us, our lives would change overnight. If only we can live and learn from past, present experiences to open for future calculated experience with this we can become successful.

Every man is a success if you have no doubt in your mindset. The only doubt we can sometimes have is how much power we have to control our existence which is highly limited thus we should learn never to blame others who have not been able to make it as we do we should encourage others on the road that we understand more than them and thus help them to build themselves.

It is better to give than to receive but most people prefer to receive than giving. If we give, we always receive more but if we receive and receive and not give after sometime we find it difficult to receive, give always to those you know and do not know alike after all the BIBLE tells us that we all came from one family ADAM AND EVE so we are all one big family. In the world plus the world (SAND) that was used in creating us.

WHY DO PEOPLE FAIL?

Failure is a disease of the mind. People always believe in their minds that you can only achieve in life, get what you want by what you do thus most people are too occupied with working all those things that are pre suppose that the work we do completely gives us what we want kill ad destroys us emotionally. We allow dirt to pile up in our minds up to the stage that virus and germs eats away our minds to frustrations.

EXERCISES FOR THE MIND

Upon waking up in the morning

1. Sing songs of praises

2. Get a clean glass of water

3. Pray holding the glass of water

4. After prayer drink a little

5. Sprinkle a little into your house

6. Pour the remaining into the bucket of water you want to bathe with

7. Go out and attend to your daily bread

Upon finishing your chores for the day repeat before sleeping.

Read the Psalms if you have a bible and rest upon the LORD.

Make sure you have at least six hours of sleep in the night.

The fear of the LORD is the greatest weapon

LIVING WITHOUT THINKING

Most people live without thinking it is also sad to know that it is the educated ones who do most without thinking. Most men just want to do what others are doing irrespective of whether they have the means to what the other fellow is doing.

Everybody wants to be rich just like the next rich man had done to get his wealth. If he had cheated, killed, maimed, robbed or whatever. People just don't care and this is why we have the life long claim of bad events happening over and over again.

A lot of people go to school and learn nothing, a lot of people live the life again and again nothing until they die and majority of people who have learnt something never have the chance to make use of them in that, they are too busy pursuing other things.

Living without thinking is a big problem in this world and how it can be solved is just that people should just take more time to being with themselves to do this, they require solitude in a noiseless place. Now one has to do his thinking.

Think about your gain and loss; think about how to overcome past mistakes instead of making new ones. Our successes are a derivative of our past mistakes; the man who never makes mistakes never makes anything.

Let us sit down by ourselves and think what are we really good at doing instead of rushing to work in banks with B.A English or Fine Arts or History. Will I be good at Poultry, think within you, do you have the recourses for poultry, have you ever done anything about poultry before? What was your outcome? From one bird, how many did you have after two years? Think! Think!

Our faculty of thinking increases our awareness of the environment we live in. The more we let our environment diminish our rate of thinking, the more we become a slave to that environment.

Okay everybody wants to be in the big town think about the pros and cons, accommodation, eating, job seeking, proximity to work, is the work you are going to do the job you derive pleasure in or is it just a job you want to do just because it pays you money to feed yourself and wear rubbish.

Think well, it is only the great thinkers in this life that have made discoveries for us to move faster. Jets, airplanes, cars, electricity, solar energy to mention few. People think too much and believe in calendars, time, month and day of the week, hours and schedules with lots f things to do. One thing they have forgotten is that once you understand money, you will never have money problems.

It takes a minute to make money an hour to appreciate the money in your hands, a day to spend all and a lifetime to forget I was once a rich man, you hear people wailing.

All those rushing to have the best in life finally always misuse the best things and always leave them behind for the man who has taken his time to think and calculate and wait upon the LORD.

Let us always use our time of thinking for the time of useful consciousness to link us up with the divine when we do this, road opens and new ideas are stumbled upon.

Every man has equal opportunities before GOD, how far or how good are you reaching out for GOD in things you do, say, hear or think. Think yourself to be what you want, think and dream upon your thoughts, see yourself become one with your thoughts, think to gain, think of yourself doing what you really want to do, think of yourself getting what you want to get after this stop the thinking and let it go for other thoughts that will benefit the world. Everything in this world is all made to work together.

Nobody can work without the life. Even mosquitoes have a role to play in this life. Cockroaches too, so you too have a role and to see that role, you have to think of every other thing both living and non living and you have to think them as good and appreciate that we are all wonderful.

If you hate anything, then you are sending a negative thought into nature this may go on sailing for years, months but that negative thoughts will always come back to you to affect you in the negative part of your life.

So think positively, think good, see yourself having the best time of your life even though you may be living in difficulties or even in a wretched life, think of how good it will be to live in that life and be healthy, happy and enjoy it then gradually, think of the good life you want to live see yourself eating the best food, drinking the best wine, driving good cars with nice clothes, think no evil thought of bliss, think of calm and instantly, you will be connected to the divine realm by which all your dreams will start coming through.

Everything you lay your hands on will work the way you want it to work, it will be as if you had planned it before, it will be as if you had already done the work before. Now new ideas will come into your mind and you will see things you cannot see, things you had not seen before you got to this idea of thinking about goodness and oneness of life, the universe and the vanity of it all.

The only thing that makes any meaning in this life is happiness and food for the body to make it happier. Food for the body does not mean you should eat everything at once eat and let eat live and let live then you will see the future you thought you never had materializing the way you have thought about it.

After this, think of how to make everything work for you, the universe and others. Believe me you can be another Methuselah and live for 900years if you do not think of evil of anybody even your enemies, then, you will understand your purpose in life.

Experience comes with age but are you choosing from the good and right experiences or the bad ones? If you choose from the bad experiences they will hunt you till you die. If you choose from the good experiences, you will notice how well and healthy you are.

Everybody are thinking, a lot are thinking bad few are thinking good and a majority are not thinking at all, they just wake up, go to work earn salaries, spend them and go home, eat and sleep, have babies and went to death. They go to church and pray and that is all they believe to life.

LIFE IS BIGGER

Most people think that the life is evil but this is not so, the life is very good, the sun the air and rain. It is not the life that is evil; it is the seeing of evil in life that affects a lot of people and makes them evil.

When you are a baby, you came into this life with crying, and then nobody thought you how to eat, crawl and walk. If you can continue with yourself like this although it is impossible because you start to see and see and copy other actions and sometimes forget all other things because you want to do what you see but that which you see is not the real you, that was not taught to cry, eat, crawl and walk. If it was at the stage that you were taking into the school at life, you would have been brought up with the teachings of life but unfortunately there is no school of life all we have to learn from are the things we see, hear and eat. This learning takes a long time to develop us and there are just too many minorities find the right path and find it difficult to walk, only a few see the path and walk it and when they walk it, a lot of people cannot understand why they are always happy and when they tell people that life is simple and that all you need is to obey the natural laws of nature to succeed they will not understand.

NATURAL LAWS OF NATURE

1. Yesterday can be known but knowing tomorrow is impossible

2. If one plan does not work, change the plan but never the goal

3. When you fasten your attention to wisdom, you gain perfect understanding

4. If you are defeated in your mind, you are defeated everywhere

5. Do good always

6. It is better to something for nothing than to do nothing at all

7. There will be no problem of money or merchandise miss road if money and merchandise exchange at the right moment

8. A wise man bows to the inevitable once he knows it is inevitable

9. We all have our loses and we know and sometimes they crippled us but it will be stupidity if we invite another disease fro ourselves

10. No religion is more powerful than you own spirit and determination

11. Realization does not take place unless emotions are deeply involved

12. Nothing worth having ever is easy

13. We steal from ourselves more than we do from other people

14. It is better to get small money with peace of mind than get a lot with much problems

15. All men are under the sentence of death

16. Any problem without a solution is not a problem

17. **Formula for Happiness:** A Yes! A No! A straight line, A Goal to achieve! One at a time.

18. Live each day as if it is your last

19. Any man who takes up a job for the money he is paid has turned himself into a slave for the job.

20. Everyday above the ground is your best day

21. You have to defeat your greatest enemy "Yourself"

22. Always turn a disadvantage to an advantage

23. Never underestimate the power of human stupidity

24. Be conservative in what you do, be liberal in what you accept from others

25. Through violence you may murder the liar but you cannot murder the lie nor establish the truth

26. Those who wish for another life eternal are ravenous wolves who cannot satisfy their greed

27. Fear GOD all of the time

28. The sum total of most men's problems lies in the love of women and love of money, avoid it

29. There are different types of sorrow. Sex takes away a special type of sorrow and adds a greater type of sorrow

30. If beards was necessary for wisdom a he-goat will be a veritable plato.

31. GOD is very simple and spiritual too

32. Keep your counsel but remember always that GOD will not despise a contrite heart

33. No Success! No Retreat! No Surrender!

34. You have to be good to see the life good

35. Hard work and sound planning can make all kinds of dreams come true

36. Our faith are our real thoughts so if we believe in poverty and disease that is what we will get

37. GOD is life, GOD is love, you are GOD you are love

38. Your mind is center for all divine operations

39. Your life is precious no matter how wretched you have made it to be

40. There are no more mysteries once you understand GOD

41. Being yourself the example do only good and no harm to others

42. I do not know the key to success but the key to failure is trying to please everybody

43. The mirror has two faces

44. "According to your faith so be it unto you"

45. The knowledge of GOD gives us dominion over any adverse condition we may find ourselves

46. Always know that life wants to express joy through you

47. Do not ever imagine who your GOD is or what he will look like because if you do, you will only have an imaginary GOD and not a true GOD

48. We create our own future either willfully or unconsciously for better or for worse depending on the way we think

49. Brutality simply invite more brutality wickedness only invites more wickedness so please desist from brutality and wickedness

50. GOD is not a question of belief, He is a fact

51. The devil has his attractive ways too but his payments always ends up in evil

52. Experience is the name I aspire to man's past mistake, please learn from past mistakes

53. Truth is very pure simple and natural

54. Love gives itself it is not bought

55. Love gives no adventure so great on earth and more exciting as exploring one's own mind

56. All life is mystery but "He" is a slave, those who will never struggle to penetrate mysteries

57. He that falls in love with himself and everything around him will never have rivals

58. Knowledge is like a runaway horse. The more you chase, the more you crave and the more you crave the more you get.

59. When you are kind and patient all sorts of good thinking will inflame your body and soul.

60. Everything we learn is fro other people.

THINGS THAT MAKE US DERAIL FROM THE TRUE PURPOSE OF LIFE

MONEY

When we think too much of money forgetting that it is a natural thing when we place too much emphasis on the accumulation of it, we forget the right path and are dominated by the illusions that surround looking for it and knowing how to spend it.

DISEASE

The love of money leads to a disease of the mind, the more we look for it, the more we will pin our faith to it and it therefore becomes the basis of our faith. It can thus tell us to kill and we will kill for it, thus instead of becoming a fellow worker with GOD, we become his opposer believing that we will change when we get the money.

This is the greatest disease that can befall a man. The more we think of money, the more our mental, spiritual and knowledge of divine power detonates within us and it throws light back to the first temptation in the garden of Eden, for surely we shall die but not immediately after eating the forbidden fruit. Then certainty and uncertainty hits us like a plague.

ANXIETY

Anxiety for money and material things make us always fall short of so many other things we would have learnt and this makes us unhappy. Man must learn that he has been given the power to overcome all problems if he does not permit his thoughts to wander away from GOD. GOD's design for man is for his expression to us in him though doing what is true and good. Anxiety leads to disappointment.

DISAPPOINTMENT

This is what can destroy us totally because if what we expect does not express itself though the right channel that we expect life becomes miserable but what a lot of people have forgotten is that life at all times expresses job through us because we are here on earth for that purpose. Disappointments always lead to discouragement.

DISCOURAGEMENT

When we are discouraged, we become a failure; discouragement has leaded a lot of people to commit suicide and to insanity.

Discouragement is what leads a lot people from not believing in GOD as our never failing father. Discouragement leads to fear.

FEAR

Fear has been defined as the biggest devil of all. It is the greatest destructive element that one can entertain of heaven or hell, fear of this fear of that.

Fear is nothing but an imagination fighting against the will, don't fear, fear. Fear thus leads to self-condemnation.

SELF-CONDEMNATION

Once we reach this stage, we become too weak to continue with life and assume it that well this is all I can become. There is no other way out, we become failures, we refuse to think of a way out of our present circumstance refuses us to make us move forward and we blame life for all the bad things happening to us forgetting that we are the ones that invited it upon ourselves. We start to think of injustice and our mental and spiritual records and lives with abject failure in poverty.

Self-condemnation is a very unpleasant condition. It is a continually an unhappy state of mind that results from viewing life from the standpoint of view of failure.

To get out of all this derailment of life, our perfect reflection of who GOD is must be known. When we know who GOD is, we become GOD ourselves and if we desire to be like GOD, we should avoid entirely in thought, feeling and understanding of what we said to gain, if we believe in the laws of nature and who advocated them. This ideas put to cognitive uses will bring peace and self esteem of all times.

May all those who believe in GOD truly never have damnation?

HIGH SENSITIVENESS

The mind becomes highly sensitive when we think of something and do not get the right answer in the way we want it or when life or man displeases us. We should never be selfish in our thoughts because whatever we think nature is coming back to us so we should be liberal in what we think and what we say to others. A continually happy state is what is needed for a continually happy living drawing all knowledge from the bible. Life is not just a system by which we can just draw up all we need all of the time through prayers alone it is faith that can win us all things.

As the past will never be repeated, others who did not participate can never know it. No matter how fast you run the past is always behind you and the more things change the more they remain the same, so I suggest that you should never let others decide for you, what to do create your own image that will command attention so as not to bore people doing this you create a high sensitiveness.

If you intend to be rich in this world, you have to be like a chameleon changing colors at different intervals assuming any type of shape, flexible and always concealing a part of you that will reveal the knowledge that you have. Should learn to say a lot by saying little if you ever accept the role that people want to pay then you are doomed because without a good weapon a wise man cannot fight his enemy and win.

The reputation of a wise man depends solely on what he concealed rather than what he shows to other people. Like this, a true man conceals his mistakes when he makes one.

I would rather betray my enemy than let my enemy betray me in the forest, the straight trees are cut down while the crooked ones are left standing, so you should never be too straight forward in this life.

Do you know why people work so hard? It is because they are weak, incompetent and have to put an extra effort to keep up with the pace of living.

Brother take your leisure, save energy think and don't ever be in a hurry at least you know that your life is in stages you learnt to crawl, walk talk. Always find the right people to do your work for you. I will never do the hard work that others can do for me because I always think ahead and bait others into doing the wok for me.

People who always think they are too wise are always the most stupid. People who calculate too much are prone to entering difficulties they never imagined possible so please if you do not know or are sure of the course of an action do not go ahead with the action.

In a problem, situation, people get confused easily seeing options where there are no options thereby crating more problems for themselves. If you ever enter into action without enough total confidence, you set up a block in your own path without realizing it. The bold draws attention and whatever draws attention, draws power.

When you are small and unnoticed you look for a goliath to attack. The bigger the goliath, the more attention you gain.

In this world, only a few can think beyond the present and not that any man who carries his triumphs too far will set his own road to decline so if you have made yourself known do not push it too far and always have an alternative because your plans must always include an alternative to be able to deal with sudden twists and shifts of fortune.

If any man tells you that he knows the source of GOD's power, he is a liar. Nobody knows the source of GOD's power we only see the effects in what we do or see in this world. Always let others think that you are stupid avoid showing others how clever you are it is always clever to conceal how clever you truly are.

Don't ever let anyone fathom the limits of your ideas always appear to be the only one that does what you do and because you always achieve your accomplishments with ease, people will always think that you can do more than what you really do.

Most people of this world do not always know that themselves created their problems instead of seeing the rose flower they only see the thorns. They always blame other people, GOD or believe it is their destiny. GOD never created any man to be poor.

Your high sensitiveness will carry you high. Do not ever if you want to tell a lie tell one that will not be believed so it is always better to tell the truth.

It is better to tell lies that will be believed than to tell the truth that will not be believed.

Every man has a weakness. If you are looking for suckers, look for the unhappy and dissatisfied. The simple are happier and have lesser problems than the rich and the powerful to content at all times. People in a hurry to get what they want always lose their self control on the long run.

Keeping your cool and having patience using the power of time to strike, your timing will never fail you. When success is built up slowly, it lasts slowly but when it is built up fast it ends fast.

Always ignore those things that you know are impossible to attain, the less interest you have on an impossible matter, the bigger the boss you are to the impossible sensitiveness.

GENEROSITY

Generosity is a strategic weapon to building your influence in the sense that, if you give something to another, he feels indebted to you and you have become the recipient's superior.

Waste a little of your fortune so that you can strategically win people's heart and make them indebted to you forever. You should note that anything given to you for free is dangerous to collect. It is always wise to pay the full price than looking for a short cut. It is better to give than to receive. Be frugal with your own money this will attract more people to you.

When you show you cool when others are mad at you, it unsettles them. Anger only shows how weak you are. When you keep your head when others lose theirs, you turn their toss to your own advantage.

It is always tactical to lure your opponents into action first the first action reveals what the end of the action will be like. When you have to bargain or are offered something for free always know that what is involved is a psychological price tag. Always give when you want to collect more from people.

The worth of money is not in gathering a lot of it but in making use of it to your own advantage. There is enough money in this world to go round everybody but greed is the father of all problems. Money made suddenly does not last as it does not have a solid foundation, so plan, think and execute.

Your generosity will become strategic if you distract the recipients view from the real cause of the giving because recipients of gifts cannot help loving you.

Loosen the soil before you plant the seeds, it is we humans who created money and placed too much value on it. The more you can give pleasure to others with your money the more others will admire and respect you.

If you study human nature you will find out that the miser finds no comforter and whosoever wants real friends must do so by giving free gifts. The desire to get something for nothing always appears more original than what comes after.

People should learn that you could never get something for nothing, after a bad time good time follows.

SUCCESS

Once success comes your ways run away and find new friends or learn strategies deflection make little sacrifices to your old friends otherwise you should fear your old friends who will start to envy you. Anybody that attributes your success to luck is your enemy.

Success always comes with envy. Distracting those who envy you with another harmful vice makes them to leave you alone. Show your wealth only in your pocket.

Anyone who praises you continually envies you, so destroy the weed of envy by not giving them anything to eat, do not ever help those that envy you otherwise they will think you are condemning them.

Once you know that someone envies you display more to them so that they can envy you more but be careful never leave a careless door open for them to use as an opportunity to nail you to a cross like this, they will be trapped and cannot harm.

The trumpet that sounds for the envied is always a death for the person who envies. The punishment of his heart can only bring misery to his life every time he hears about the success of the person he envies.

Good luck and success is more dangerous than bad luck. Bad luck is a teacher while good luck plays strange tricks on the mind especially when you are envied. Do not play with fire except and unless you have prepared for it not to burn you.

Our opinion of GOD and our knowledge of man than one can conclude that it is a generality and necessary law of nature to rule over whatever one can so do not ever be deceived that as a poor man, you can be a friend of the rich man or as a fool the friend of the wise or as a coward the friend of the courageous and brave.

It is only two men of equal standards that can be friendly with each other, a fool and a fool will always play together, the rich and the rich always flock together while the coward makes friends with a coward like himself.

When you end up relying on other people ideas, you end up not being able to make new ideas for yourself. The greatest question about life is to always ask yourself, why people are wicked knowing fully well that wickedness does not pay.

I even have a friend who gave himself the nickname WICKED.

Being honest in this world is not a good thing because honesty at all times offends people. Any man who wants to be good at all times is only fooling himself. Deception is a tool that one must make use of at certain intervals and it must be used over and over because majority of the world do not want the truth. If we do not have enemies around us, we grow careless and carefree but with enemies surrounding us we grow focused and alert.

Repaying gratitude to a man is burdensome but revenge is always pleasurable so always guide people towards the wrong path so that they can never know your real intentions and so harm you. If they do not know what you are up to they will leave you alone. When people know you in and out they will not respect you telling people what they want to hear is what count making yourself honest you become predictable and become an easy access to harm and this is why people with power always track honesty by concealing their real intentions always know how to win your wars before the battle.

People who preach revolution always fight with arms and those with the powerful reaction with the revolution to fight back with arms both ways the two are the same people. Revolution always ends up with the same things of the past that necessitated it to come to pass. The change that comes with revolution always creates another opening for the past to come back.

Generosity becomes strategic only when it distracts the recipients view from the real cause of giving because you should always know that recipients of gifts no matter how small cannot help loving you.

Always till your soil before planting your seeds. It is humans who created money and placed too much importance and value on it but the more you can give pleasure to others with your money, the more others will admire and respect you. If you study nature you will find out that the miser always find no comforter and whoever wanted to make friends must do so by giving, givers never lack.

Remember always that the role people want you to play in this world may not be the role you actually want to play. You can always create your own role and live the role that best befits your imagination and those of other people.

The more you are more comfortable with your own role the more natural you become and move on the ladder of success. You can never help being what you are so be genuine all of us are liars so know that salvation can only come to those who have gone astray and ask for forgiveness. Behave like a blank screen while moving through life, never let people see the real you otherwise they will seize you and consume you always turn your face like the television making it bright with contrast and colour.

A role may look charismatic, it played the right way but charisma depends on success so to be practical and cautious when you turn your image and presence, people will you as superior and worthy of imitation.

People who worship idols see what they want to see in the idol because their god the idol lives in their imagination but the idol is just a piece of wood joined together.

If you set a trap with something sweet and attractive it makes the prey blind to the danger that lies ahead. Use honesty only when you want to disarm your enemies because who can distrust a man caught in the action of being honest. Your reputation serves you an aura that brings respect for setting you apart from other people when your reputation smells honesty then you can make people do things for you by deceiving then at all levels.

THIS BOOK IS ONLY FOR MEN

The men they fancy themselves, they have never come to realize that it is the woman that hold power.

Do not ever think that the woman is the tender creature we are meant to believe, majority of them are evil in nature and therefore the most dangerous of things in life.

Most people never tend to talk or write about the woman because most men are fools and the women tends to lead them down a path men already know like this, the man never realize that the woman is leading him into a trap.

The more things change the more they remain the same, the first woman brought sin into the world, couples still indulge in courting rituals, women still kiss their husbands and kill them.

No matter how fast you run, the woman is always in front of the man. Any man who cannot control himself with a woman cannot control himself or others. The woman is a wild animal that is not easy to tame just like your tongue.

When the night falls, the woman dazzle men with the cover of the night with different types of beauty but any man who is deceived will only find woe in the end. So always concentrate your forces of control on the woman like this you will always be the master of any woman you meet. Never let your mind stray as a man whenever you're with a woman concentrate on what you want from the woman.

Is it love, is it children, is it sex? What do you actually want? Most people say that behind every successful man there is a woman. In most cases it is a lie but if the woman is reliable it may be so and this is why most successful men are worse than the devil.

People who think that women are very good creative, loving, sexy need to have their heads examined. Desire for the woman often creates paradoxical effects on the man. The more you want the woman the more you chase after her and she on her own side deceives you by making you think she is eluding you this makes you show more interest, the more interest you show the more the woman acknowledges your actions and thus because your interest is so strong, the woman turns her back on you and makes you weak by ignoring you. Without women, you cancel a lot of unhappiness out of your life but the more you respond to their whims and fallacies the more you become partners of sorts each moving in step to actions and reactions that contradict the process that the man thought will lead to happiness like this, the man looses the initiative and opens himself to the influence of the woman like this the man is made to sin against himself and against his GOD his creator.

Go ye into the world is a curse for man for disobeying GOD had he listened he would have stayed in the Garden of Eden forever without dying but for every action there is a reaction with the woman you can test your capabilities, your strength and your faith and belief in GOD. With woman men get confused easily seeing things they are not supposed to see, seeing options where there are no options thereby creating more problems for themselves.

If you ever go after a woman without the guidance of GOD, you create your own unhappiness with your own eyes. Seek ye the moon in a woman and you will find yourself fighting with a tiger.

Try as much as possible to meet with different types of women, try as much possible to make friends with them, if you do not have women as friends women will fail you woefully but once you know them, then you can use them to your advantage and they will respect you. If at all you want to be honest with a woman let it be deceptive because the woman of the world today and yesterday can only thrive and live on deception so be cunning as a man with a woman never let a woman know your heart.

Do not ever be afraid of women, any man who knows his woman well will know what he is fighting against and thus he can prepare for whatever the woman wants to do against or for him.

The women from the onset from creation have been bad creatures from Eve to Jacob's wives to Moses' wife to Samson and Delilah to Solomon and his Queen women have always deceived men thereby leading to their downfall.

If you at all want to be honest with a woman in this world. If you want to be honest with yourself first put aside your ego that they are our mothers.

Majority of women are evil so if you want to deal with a woman either by loving her or cherishing her in this life lead her down a path she already knows like this she will never know that you are leading her into a trap once your trap catches her she will know who she is fighting against and once she know who she fighting against, she will succumb to your wishes and even with this you still have to be cautious and never leave your backdoor open for her because she will catch you unawares and still betray you or lead you to the only road they know for men. MEN DOWNFALL

If a man concentrates in his mind to want to tame the Devil he will always succeed because men were created in the image of GOD.

Always concentrate your forces on your woman's weakest spot and because they are necessary evils the master the woman will serve the slave who is the man.

It is always better in the life of a man never to overstep his bounds doing what he sees others doing because they are doing it. If a man thinks that showing love or giving too much love to a woman will make the woman love him the man is overstepping his bounds as all men who toil and work for the woman have sold themselves into slavery. Do not ever let your woman decide what to do for you. Create you own image and that will command attention and a woman will never catch you unaware.

Women have always been the center of attraction for men but even the bible states that it is better for men not to marry but that if a man decides to marry, he should find a good woman to live the rest of his life with. Well if you really want to live the rest of your life with a good woman of your choice I have no objection but from the beginning women have been admiring the clean hands of their honest husbands' graves. One has to soil his hands sometimes to make them clean don't ever in this world trust a woman trust your own instincts.

When you pick up a woman for better for worse, the man is always on the loosing side when you start courting the man is at the loosing side it is the man who spends and spends when they marry, it is still the man that provides everything always on the loosing side when you have children, it is the man that send them to school, feeds and clothes then when their children grow up it is their mother they respect more than the man.

The mother poisons their heart against their father at all times the man is the loser because those children he claims are his are their mothers.

Majority of the men in this world are docile and dull rejecting the truth with equal lack of positive reason. They are blind in that they are a friend with the world and thus they become an enemy of GOD what I am saying is pure truth and simple truth I do not say that it will always be obvious but there is nothing so mysterious and sublime as simplicity, a man who knows the truth is not dogmatic as a hunger for love and comradeship is as natural to our species as requirement for food and water.

When a man hands are full of money it is natural for women to surface some will drop from the sky as rain. A great fortune has been lost to them by idiots and fools who made that money.

Sometimes I think "forget about the love crap and enjoy myself get all the ass I can while still young, fuck women and run like this, you can never get hurt but if I kept daydreaming about love, I'll only go on making a complete fool of myself, a complete goddamned fool out of myself over and over again until the woman will plant me in the ground for the seed I am".

After all why do I want to bring another child into this bad world to go over the bad things bad life bad people I've seen and mixed with?

If one sits down in this world and think. If you think there's really something called love if you really want to be honest with yourself believe there's actually a thing called love, as strong as the word and as real as it sounds what you are doing to yourself is setting up yourself for a lot of pain. It is a lie when people talk about love it is a big lie love is something writers invented to sell their books only GOD is love when you believe in HIM and put all your totality in him.

The question I'm putting to men now is what they should be asking themselves now are they enjoying marriage? Marriage is a sorry end for any man who wants to enjoy his freedom.

The sum total of men's problems in this world lies in women and love of money. Are not all women troublemakers? And they come in three categories those that want to kill the man and acquire his wealth with children, those that are really scared of life and want someone a man to feed them and the prostitutes who do not care about any man, they are ruthless all they want is money.

Do not ever be trapped with the woman's feminine mystique all woman are two faces tramps. Sex is one thing a man does not absolutely have to understand, it's like looking at the sea and studying the fish, studying all animals but with all the guilt attached to it, it is in a position of indispensable necessity, which one must be especially careful of.

There is only one true love GOD but there are over one hundred and eighty million photocopies the woman.

Courtship situation as earlier mentioned is like purchase situation, if you do not have what the woman wants the woman will bullshit you the woman too is in a selling situation. If you do not have what to offer she herself does not have what to sell. Love and sex should be savored and not rushed into.

Adam had a peaceful existence in the Garden of Eden until he was deceived by Eve with a golden apple. The difference between a mother and a wife is that one brings you into the world crying while the other never leaves you without crying both from the beginning of your life she makes you cry.

To win on a chess board you have to get your opponent react to the false moves you make by keeping him on the defensive when you do this he will eventually make a mistake then you can go for a mate. This is a good strategy if you really want to live with a woman make them come to you then you will be in control otherwise carry your load and run or the other way round get your love then run.

I AM SINGLE BECAUSE MARRIAGE IS NOT REAL, I AM SINGLE BECAUSE TOO MANY LIES ARE INVOLVED, I AM SINGLE BECAUSE IT WASTES MY TIME, MY FREEDOM AND MY MONEY I AM SINGLE BECAUSE I AM ALWAYS THE LOOSER WORKING FOR WHAT I WILL NEVER GET. ILL ALWAYS REMAIN SINGLE BECAUSE I WAS SINGLE WHEN I CAME INTO LIFE.

FRIEND/TRUST

Your enemy always is not from another country or speaks another language, it is your father, and cousin or a man or woman you used to know well and sometimes it could be your own brother or the woman you love. Who can you trust today? The man you trust today may kill you tomorrow.

I believe in the promises of others like the air I breath/suck in with my mouth it gives me the satisfaction of taking in too much air and without making me unhappy.

Although risk may be a precondition of reward, people are as complicated as you can think. They wear masks to conceal their real intentions; it takes a minute to find a friend it takes some time to appreciate them but a lifetime to forget the hurt they give you.

All of us like actors on the stage people can never know what you are thinking or feeling. They can only judge you on your appearance, which is deceptive. As most people only judge by what they see, everybody is making use of everybody to survive.

In this world some people hunt animals while some hunt humans like themselves to make a living while some hunt what others have hunted. It is always better to be a vulture so as to save yourself from a lot of hardship. The vulture is a patient bird of prey.

Knowledge of people how they live and interact is what improves your judgment of them. Self interest is a disease of men but knowledge of people increases your way of living with them most men know where they are but not why.

The world is full of Godless and wretched men one bastard dies today and another bastard is born to replace him, don't ever try to get the good side of another man because there is no limit to the stupidity of men.

It is so strange that those who wish all men to be kind are themselves incapable of showing kindness. what a world so weak, so whimpering, so greedy, so exigent, so fearful, so heedless of history, so brutal and sentimental and filthy with infinitude of crimes perpetuated on the body and mind.

Whether foolish or strong, wise or weak, beggarly or proud a man must answer solely for himself. My ideas are my vast empire where I live happily. They may be wrong for you but they have guided me successfully and if you are reading this today you will find deeply rooted in you some truth of some sort, which you know, is the truth.

INSIDE EACH OF US ARE TWO WOLVES

ONE IS EVIL

IT IS ANGER
ENVY SORROW
REGRET GREED
ARROGANCE
SELF PITY
GUILT
RESENTMENT
INFERIORITY
LIES
FALSE PRIDE
SUPERIORITY
AND EGO

ONE IS GOOD

IT IS JOY
PEACE LOVE
HOPE
SERENITY
HUMILITY
KINDNESS
BENEVOLENCE
EMPATHY
GENEROSITY
TRUTH
COMPASSION
AND FAITH

© Blu222

WHICH WOLF WINS? THE ONE YOU FEED MOST